MORE BULLETIN BOARDS FOR EVERY MONTH

JEANNE CHEYNEY
ARNOLD CHEYNEY

Good Year Books

DEDICATION

To Teachers of Children Everywhere

Good Year Books
are available for most basic curriculum subjects plus many enrichment areas. For more Good Year Books, contact your local bookseller or educational dealer. For a complete catalog with information about other Good Year Books, please write to

Good Year Books
P.O. Box 91858
Tucson, AZ 85752-1858
www.goodyearbooks.com

Design: Meyers Design
Cover Illustration: Meyers Design
Interior Illustration: Jeanne Cheyney

ISBN-10 1-59647-013-5
ISBN-13 978-1-59647-013-2
4 5 6 7 8 9 - MCG - 09 08 07 06

CONTENTS

CONTENTS

CONTENTS

INTRODUCTION

More Bulletin Boards for Every Month is designed for teachers of children in kindergarten through third grade, but teachers in other grades and subject areas will also find useful ideas. Each bulletin board has patterns that may be used as guides. Taken together, these bulletin boards cover many curriculum areas.

The following suggestions will make your bulletin boards appealing and easier to construct.

1. In a very short time, you will learn which students can cut and color well in your class, so let them help with the artwork for the bulletin boards. Explain the directions and they'll enjoy helping.

2. Bulletin boards are made attractive by brilliant coloring. Pressing heavily on crayons when coloring the bulletin board display items will help eliminate a "washed-out" look.

3. Solid-colored cloth for bulletin board backgrounds can be washed and used many times. A light-colored background may make it difficult for some items to show up well. Outline such items with dark, broad-tipped markers or place contrasting dark paper behind them, if needed.

4. Within the Instructions for each bulletin board, you will find research information for introducing topics to be taught.

5. Use scrap paper from the office copier, as long as one side is clean.

6. One simple way to attach items to the bulletin board or the surrounding wall is to roll a piece of transparent tape sticky side out around your finger until it overlaps, press it where an item is to be placed, and attach the item to it. Larger items can be attached in the same way by using wide, clear shipping tape. The two tapes stick well to most surfaces.

7. Figures and other items can go beyond the bulletin board itself. Think of your blank walls as potential display surfaces too.

MATERIALS AND SUPPLIES

- dark-green cloth background
- white border
- white letters
- wide, clear shipping tape
- crayons
- any white paper that crayons can write on
  (Used computer paper, clean on one side, is OK.)
- scissors
- glue

INSTRUCTIONS

1. Prepare bulletin board for the first day of school, if desired.
2. Use the boy or girl patterns on pages 101 and 102. (Follow solid lines for boy's hair and dotted lines for girl's hair.) Glue the body parts together at the dotted lines. Color the girl's shirt yellow with a red flower (page 100) and her shorts red with yellow flowers. In-line skates are red. Her hair is bright orange. The boy's hair is black and his cap bright blue and white. The shirt is bright blue, the shorts bright orange, and the in-line skates bright blue. Use heavy color.
3. Pencils, page 73, and crayons, page 75, are bright blue, green, and red.
4. Use any bright-colored paper for the two books. Fold papers in half widthwise.
5. Using the pattern on page 110, cut outlines of in-line skates for children's name tags for the first days of school.
6. Let each child draw a skating figure to look like himself or herself. Tape these to the walls around the room.

MATERIALS AND SUPPLIES

- dark-green cloth background
- orange border
- orange letters
- any brown, white, and tan paper that crayons can write on
- 3 or 4 sheets of lined primary paper
- 3/4″ transparent tape
- crayons
- scissors

INSTRUCTIONS

1. This bulletin board can be used to welcome the children to your class on the first day of school.
2. Using patterns on pages 58 to 63, make and color as many figures as desired. Use your choice of paper for skin colors. Use heavy colors for clothes and facial features.
3. Cut two faces only for top and side of bulletin board and cut three hands from the pattern on page 56. Tape them to the wall.
4. Make crayons and pencils from the patterns on pages 73 and 75. Color heavily. Add sheets of lined primary paper.

HOW MANY CATS?
HOW MANY OF EACH COLOR?

MATERIALS AND SUPPLIES

- medium-blue cloth background
- orange borders
- black, orange, red, green, blue, purple, yellow, and brown paper (Not all colors are necessary.)
- orange letters
- scissors
- transparent tape

INSTRUCTIONS

1. Prepare a few cats or many cats, depending on grade level. Choose patterns from pages 78 and 79.
2. Place cats on the bulletin board. Tape three around the outside of the bulletin board.
3. Ask the children to count the cats. Then count the number of cats of each color. Older children can write their names and answers on scrap paper and give them to their teacher.

MATERIALS AND SUPPLIES

- bright-orange cloth background
- white typing or computer paper (amount optional)
- transparent tape
- white scrap paper (Used computer paper, clean on one side, is OK.)
- green border (edge in black if needed)
- green letters (edge in black if needed)
- wide-tipped black and green markers
- crayons
- scissors

INSTRUCTIONS

1. With the children, discuss ways to have a quiet, happy classroom. Write their ideas on the chalkboard: Don't make fun of others. Speak quietly. Work quietly. Raise your hand before speaking. Do your best work. Walk quietly in line. Be kind to others. Treat others as you want them to treat you. Be a good neighbor, and so on.
2. Print the rules with black marker on white paper; the number is optional. Outline with green marker.
3. Use the face patterns on pages 64 to 67. Let each child color a pattern to look like himself or herself and cut it out. (On pages 64 and 67, two boys' faces have dotted lines added in order to make girls' faces and hair from the same patterns. For girls' faces in these two patterns, omit the ears, if desired.)
4. Outline faces with black marker, if needed.
5. Tape faces to the edges of the bulletin board.

MATERIALS AND SUPPLIES

- dark-blue cloth background
- white border
- white letters
- wide-tipped black marker

- any white paper that crayons can write on
  (Used computer paper, clean on one side, is OK.)
- crayons
- scissors

INSTRUCTIONS

1. Discuss any manners that need attention:
   - Do I clean up classroom materials?
   - Do I answer others nicely?
   - Do I say, "Fine, thank you," if someone asks me how I am?
   - Do I quietly wait for my turn?
   - Do I put playthings away?
   - Do I talk with my mouth full of food?
   - Do I treat others, including my family, as I want them to treat me?
   - If a friend gives me a cookie, do I say, "Thank you"?
   - Do I say "Please" if I want something?
   - Do I say "Excuse me" if I bump someone?
   - If I cough or sneeze, do I cover my mouth or nose with my hand or tissue?
2. Encourage the children, two at a time, to act out these situations and show appropriate responses.
3. Using patterns on pages 64 to 67, color and cut out faces.
4. On scrap computer paper, cut rectangles 8¹/₂″ by 5¹/₂″. Using the marker, print these sentences:
   - I clean up classroom materials.
   - I eat with my mouth closed.
   - I put playthings away.
   - I say "Excuse me."
   - I say "Please."
   - I say "Thank you."
5. Let the children draw and color pictures of the good manners listed in #4.
6. Follow up this activity by encouraging children to say "please," "thank you," and "excuse me."

MATERIALS AND SUPPLIES

- black background
- white border
- white letters
- colored paper (optional)
- white paper pieces (for the "juggling" path)

- any white paper that crayons can write on
  (Used computer paper, clean on one side, is OK.)
- crayons
- scissors
- glue

INSTRUCTIONS

1. Ask the children to name as many fruits as they can. Write them on the chalkboard:
   apples, apricots, avocados, bananas, blackberries, blueberries, cantaloupes, cranberries, dates, elderberries, grapes, grapefruit, kiwi, lemons, mangoes, oranges, papayas, peaches, pears, pineapples, plums, raspberries, rhubarb, star fruit, strawberries, tangerines, watermelons
2. Talk about the importance of eating fruits each day for good health.
3. Ask the children to name favorite fruits and why they like them.
4. Discuss things made from fruits: juices, jams, sauces, pies, dried fruit, sherbet, ice cream, jellies, fruitcake, salads, cookies, and so on.
5. Using the patterns on pages 93, 103, and 110, cut fruits from scrap computer paper and color heavily, or use colored paper.
6. Use the boy pattern on page 96. Color as desired and glue shoes on legs at dotted lines. Use white paper for the "juggling path" between plums.
7. Bring in a variety of fruits. Cut them in half. Study the seeds. Offer children samples to taste (of course, first check with parents concerning food allergies).

MATERIALS AND SUPPLIES

- medium-blue cloth background
- dark-blue cloth background inside the house
- transparent tape
- dark-blue border
- dark-blue letters
- light-green cloth or paper
- assorted colored paper
- white computer or typing paper
  (Used computer paper, clean on one side, is OK.)
- brown grocery bags
- crayons
- scissors
- glue

INSTRUCTIONS

1. Ask children what they do to help at home. Stress the importance of everyone doing something to help with family duties. Promise a bulletin board surprise for the following day. Tell the children to be ready to color pictures of themselves helping at home:

    take out garbage, take a bath when told, hang clothes on hangers, go to bed when told, pick up toys and things, help with laundry, sweep, mop, dust, wash dishes, turn off lights, feed and walk pets, put dishes away, set the table, play with the baby, make school lunch, put bicycle away, make beds

2. On a table or on the floor, lay dark-blue cloth or paper approximately the size of your desired house.
3. Cut $1/2''$ wide strips of white paper for partitions and floors for the house (number of rooms optional). Full-size rooms are $7''$ high by $11''$ wide, inside measurements. Glue strips together to form rooms, tape them to the dark-blue cloth or paper, and cut off anything left over. Attach the house to the bulletin board.
4. Cut light-green cloth or paper, or grocery bags painted green for the yard and tree crowns.
5. For the roof, cut $1''$ wide strips from a grocery bag.
6. Using patterns on pages 111, 112, 113, 114, and 115, cut house furniture from light-brown paper or grocery bags. Tape the furniture pieces in the rooms.
7. Using the pattern on page 113, cut windows $2''$ by $4''$ from white paper. Color curtains. Tape one in each room.
8. After the house is prepared, give the children one of the child patterns from page 113. Let the children color these patterns to look like themselves doing special jobs at home. On pages 113 and 115 are patterns for toys, dust cloth, pet food, hangers, mop, broom, garbage bag, and so on; use these, or let the children draw these things themselves.

MATERIALS AND SUPPLIES

- bright-yellow cloth background
- black border
- black letters
- red, black, and white paper
- broad-tipped black marker
- transparent tape
- any white paper that crayons can write on
  (Used computer paper, clean on one side, is OK.)
- crayons
- scissors
- glue

INSTRUCTIONS

1. Discuss the color red or any color of your choice.
2. Ask the children to cut something of that color from magazines or newspapers for the bulletin board.
   (Can labels or bits of yarn or ribbon are possibilities too.)
3. Cut a front view of a red Danny Dibby and parts from the patterns on page 76. Cut black-and-white caps from the pattern on page 77, or color black parts with crayons. Glue arms, legs, and caps in place.
4. If needed, outline Danny and parts with black marker.
5. Make Danny's eyes, nose, and mouth from black or white paper, whichever shows up better. Black marker can be used too.
6. Cut four red hands from the arm and hand pattern on page 76.
7. Place Danny Dibby parts around the bulletin board.

MATERIALS AND SUPPLIES

- black cloth background
- red apple border
- red letters
- red and green paper (optional)
- white computer paper (amount optional)
- broad-tipped black marker
- any white paper that crayons can write on (Used computer paper, clean on one side, is OK.)
- transparent tape
- crayons
- scissors
- glue

INSTRUCTIONS

1. Talk with the children about special class duties: erasing chalkboard, passing papers, leading lines, cleaning up, passing the wastebasket, handing out books, and so on.
2. Use the apple pattern on page 62 to cut enough red apples with green leaves and stems to go around your bulletin board, or use white paper and color apples heavily. Tape apples in place.
3. As an option, trace around your hand and use various colors of hands for a border.
4. Fold computer paper nearly in half, lengthwise, and glue the ends together. (These make pockets for children's duties.)
5. Cut enough white paper slips, 9″ by 7″, for each child's name so that when it's his or her turn for a class duty you can put a slip with the child's name on it in the pocket for that duty.
6. Change names each week.

MATERIALS AND SUPPLIES

- medium-blue cloth background
- black border
- black letters
- black, brown, orange, yellow, and red paper (optional)
- black, brown, orange, yellow, and red paints (optional)
- wide-tipped black marker for labels

- any white paper that crayons can write on (Used computer paper, clean on one side, is OK.)
- brown grocery bags (optional)
- felt-tipped black pen
- crayons
- scissors
- glue

INSTRUCTIONS

1. Ask the children how we get ready for winter. We get out our warm clothes, boots, warm blankets, and so on.
2. Ask the children how animals get ready for winter. Some eat more food with fat in it (nuts and seeds). Many animals grow thicker fur. Birds fluff their feathers on cold days. Some animals store food in underground holes where they sleep. Some animals hibernate (sleep through the cold winter). Squirrels dig holes and bury nuts.
3. Point out that trees and plants also get ready for winter. The leaves change color and drop off so the trees and plants can rest for the winter. Some plants die and new ones come up in spring.
4. Cut four tree crowns, two orange, one yellow, and one red, from the pattern on page 85. Use colored paper, white paper and crayons, or grocery bags and paints. Place an orange crown on the left, then a yellow, a red, and another orange at the right.
5. Cut four brown tree trunks from the pattern on page 61. Use colored paper, white paper colored brown, or grocery bags and paints.
6. Make a brown squirrel (without the dotted line), page 88; a brown and black raccoon, page 111; a brown chipmunk with brown stripes down the back and tail, page 74; and a red or blue bird, page 112. Make the animals with colored paper, white paper and crayons, or grocery bags and paints.
7. Using seed and nut patterns on pages 111 and 112, make a dark-brown walnut, light-brown hickory nut, dark-brown chestnut with light-brown center spot, brown acorn, light-brown walnut, medium-brown hazelnut, black sunflower seeds, and yellow corn. Outline each seed and nut with black pen for accent.
8. Place a yellow or orange strip of paper behind the rows of nuts or seeds to make them more visible.
9. Put acorns, corn, and sunflower seeds on the ground.

MATERIALS AND SUPPLIES

- medium-blue cloth background
- orange border
- orange letters
- pink, purple, orange, black, yellow, and green paper (optional)

- any white paper that crayons can write on (Used computer paper, clean on one side, is OK.)
- crayons
- scissors
- glue

INSTRUCTIONS

1. Prepare bulletin board items from patterns on pages 73, 74, and 107. Color items heavily or use colored paper.
2. Ask the children to name the shapes in each figure.
3. Point to each item again and let the children count the number of shapes in each.
4. Cut ovals, circles, squares, triangles, rectangles, half circles, quarter circles, diamonds, and so on. Let the children build creative shapes at their tables or desks and glue them on white paper.

MATERIALS AND SUPPLIES

- medium-blue cloth background
- black border
- black letters
- transparent tape

- wide-tipped black marker
- crayons
- scissors

INSTRUCTIONS

1. Make a photocopy of the sailing ship and figures on pages 104 and 105. (Do not cut out the ship.) Color the figures as desired.
2. Make the cross red and the water and sky blue.
3. Tape pages 102 and 103 together, making sure the sail lines come together.
4. Outline the entire picture with black marker.
5. Encourage the children to read books, especially stories that took place long ago. Simple biographies of famous people in history are good reading for the children who can read. Spark their interest by reading a simple biography to the class. (See *People of Purpose,* published by Good Year Books.)

WHAT IS A PUMPKIN?

MATERIALS AND SUPPLIES
- black cloth background
- white border
- orange letters
- yellow, orange, and green paper (optional)
- brown grocery bags (optional)
- yellow, orange, and green paints (optional)
- computer paper
- any white paper that crayons can write on
  (Used computer paper, clean on one side, is OK.)
- wide-tipped black marker
- transparent tape
- crayons
- scissors
- glue

INSTRUCTIONS
1. Cut orange pumpkins (amount optional) from the pattern on page 69. You can also cut them from white paper and color heavily or cut them from grocery bags and paint them orange.
2. Using the pumpkin vine pattern on page 70, cut from green paper, from white paper and color heavily, or from grocery bags and paint the parts green.
3. Cut the yellow flower from the pattern on page 70, or cut from white paper and color heavily or from grocery bags and paint yellow. Glue stem, leaf, and flower to the pumpkin.
4. With crayons, color red ridges on the pumpkin.
5. Place one or more pumpkins on the bulletin board and extend parts beyond if desired. (The pumpkin, lower left, is reversed.)
6. Ask the children where pumpkins grow, or assign the question to the children and have them ask their parents.
7. Some pumpkin facts: They are vegetables, grow in patches in fields, are planted in June, ripen in September or October, are used for cattle food, are stringy inside, have many seeds and a tough skin, and have yellow flowers and prickly leaves and stems. They are used for pies (take out the stringy insides and seeds, cut off the tough skin, and cook the thick fleshy part that is left).
8. Cut four sheets of white computer paper in half lengthwise for eight labels. With the marker, write these words:

    a vegetable, tough skin, many seeds, many prickly leaves, yellow flowers, grow in fields, cattle food, pies

MATERIALS AND SUPPLIES

- black cloth background
- orange border
- orange letters
- eight 5″ by 8″ cards
- bulletin board space within reach of children

- 16 letter-size envelopes, $3^1/2$″ by $6^1/2$″
- 32 thumb tacks
- crayons
- scissors
- glue

INSTRUCTIONS

1. Use the patterns on page 99 for the boy, hand, and question mark. Color and cut.
2. Turn the flaps of the letter-size envelopes backward and glue them to the back of the envelope.
3. Tack the envelopes to the bulletin board (two tacks at the top of each). Place them on the lower part of the bulletin board in two, three, or four rows so the children can reach them.
4. Cut the 5″ by 8″ cards in half so each is 4″ by 5″.
5. Print eight sets of matching words on the sixteen cards.
6. Write important words from any subject you want to reinforce, including health, science, reading, spelling, and social studies.

7. For kindergarten, match pairs of colors, numbers, beginning sounds, and so on.
8. Mix your sixteen words (eight matching pairs) and place one word in each of the sixteen envelopes. Turn the cards so only the blank sides show.
9. Divide your class into two teams. Let a child from one team come up and turn any two cards around. Hold them up for the class to see where they are located in their envelopes. If the two cards match, the child gets a point for his or her team. The matching cards are then placed in the envelopes so the class can see the words. If the two cards do not match, the child puts them back in the two envelopes, with the blank sides showing.
10. A child from the other team comes up and turns any two cards around. Continue this procedure until all the cards are matched.
11. The team with the most pairs matched is the winner. Repeat the same game or use eight new sets of words.
12. If eight sets of words are too many, use fewer sets for each game.

WHY DO LEAVES CHANGE COLORS?

MATERIALS AND SUPPLIES
- medium-blue cloth background
- black border
- black letters
- autumn leaves
- black, yellow, red, orange, and brown paints (optional)
- black, yellow, red, orange, and brown paper (optional)
- any white paper that crayons can write on (Used computer paper, clean on one side, is OK.)
- brown grocery bags (optional)
- wide, clear shipping tape
- transparent tape
- crayons
- scissors
- glue

INSTRUCTIONS

1. Bring colored leaves to class. See if the children can name the trees from which they came.
2. Ask the children why leaves change color in autumn. Trees make chlorophyll in the spring. Chlorophyll makes leaves green. In September or October, trees stop making chlorophyll and the leaves change to other colors.
3. Discuss ways to use colored leaves. Place colored leaves between two pieces of waxed paper. Press with an iron on permanent-press setting until the waxed papers fuse together. Use leaves for mulch. Pile leaves in heaps and jump into them. Walk in leaves and listen to them crackle.
4. For a large tree, place together six sheets of 9″ by 12″ black paper lengthwise. Overlap each piece of black paper 1/2″ for gluing. Glue two lengthwise sheets of 9″ by 12″ black paper for tree base. Overlap the two black pieces 1/2″ and glue to the bottom end of the tree.
5. As an option, use two large brown grocery bags. Cut down the back seams and cut off the bottoms. Open the two bags and glue the long pieces together at the ends, overlapping 1″. Your two glued bags will be about 6′ long. Cut a tree base 12″ by 24″ from another paper bag. Glue it to the tree bottom.
6. As another option, glue three newspaper sections together to make a 6′ long strip.
7. Begin at the center top and gradually taper your tree, making it wider at the bottom. Paint the tree black, if needed. Cut it out. Trace around the top half of the tree to use as a pattern for four more branches. Trace around the top half of a branch to make four small branches. Glue branches to the tree.
8. Attach the tree to the bulletin board or wall with shipping tape.
9. Cut leaves from the patterns on pages 100 and 111. Use white paper and crayons, colored paper, or grocery bags painted various colors.
10. Cut a boy's head from the pattern on page 65. From the pattern on page 116, cut the shirt along the broken lines and glue the arms extending out to the sides. Glue the legs and feet to the boy's body. Color.
11. Tape a variety of leaves falling down and in a pile at the boy's feet.

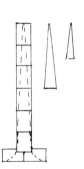

AM I A GOOD NEIGHBOR?

MATERIALS AND SUPPLIES:
- dark-green cloth background
- white border
- white letters
- white computer paper (amount optional)
- transparent tape
- any white paper that crayons can write on
  (Used computer paper, clean on one side, is OK.)
- crayons
- scissors
- glue

INSTRUCTIONS:

1. Talk with your class about the meaning of "Good Neighbors." Ask how we can be good neighbors in the classroom. The following are possible subjects for discussion.
   What happens when . . .
   I push my scraps under someone else's desk?
   I interrupt when someone is talking?
   I take things that don't belong to me?
   I am a tattletale?
   I make fun of others?
   I talk back to others?
   I push in front of others in line?
   I treat others the way I want them to treat me?
   I try to keep my things neat?
   I work quietly?
2. Discuss good-neighbor behaviors and add others, if desired.
3. Write all or some of these questions on white paper. Role-play some of the situations written on the paper.
4. Use patterns of children's faces found on pages 64 to 67 and 101. Color as desired.
5. Patterns for showing anger and sadness in mouths and eyes (front view):
   mouth for sadness, page 65; sad eyebrows, page 64; angry eyebrows, page 65; angry mouth, page 65; angry mouth and angry eye (for side view of face), pages 67 and 71. Cut each out and glue or tape the changes in mouths and eyebrows on top of the expressions already on the faces.
6. Give each child a piece of paper approximately 8″ by 10″. Ask the children to draw big faces of themselves, choosing an expression, and color it brightly. An option is to give each a pattern of a face to color. Let the children cut them out. Tape these on the wall around the bulletin board.

MATERIALS AND SUPPLIES

- medium-blue cloth background
- brown border
- brown letters
- computer paper
- brown grocery bags (optional)
- wide-tipped black or brown marker
- red, brown, orange, black, and yellow paper (optional)

- any white paper that crayons can write on (Used computer paper, clean on one side, is OK.)
- red, brown, orange, black, and yellow paints (optional)
- crayons
- scissors
- glue

INSTRUCTIONS

1. Do not put the bottom sentence under the turkeys until after the discussion with children.
2. Discuss this question: Is a turkey a bird? Ask the children what they think and why they think that way.
3. Ask children what birds have that no other animals have. (feathers)
4. Using white paper and crayons, colored paper, or grocery bags and paints, make three or more turkeys from the pattern on page 86. Make one red, one orange, and one brown. Make as many as your bulletin board can hold, if desired. Glue the legs in place.
5. Overlap the turkeys on the bulletin board.
6. Place two sheets of computer paper end-to-end. Overlap $1/2''$ and glue them together. Print these words on it: Only Birds Have Feathers.
7. Let the children draw and color their own turkeys, or give each a pattern to color.

MATERIALS AND SUPPLIES

- dark-blue cloth background
- orange letters
- orange border
- 2 toy telephones, if possible
- transparent tape
- wide-tipped black marker
- any white paper that crayons can write on
  (Used computer paper, clean on one side, is OK.)
- crayons
- scissors
- glue

INSTRUCTIONS

1. Discuss ways to talk on the telephone: Say "Hello" when answering the phone. If someone wants to talk to your mother, say, "Just a second, please." Put the phone receiver down quietly and find your mother. Tell her the call is for her. Don't hold the phone in your hand and yell for your mother to come. If your mother can't come to the phone, say, "Can you call back, please?" If you need to write down a caller's number, write it carefully. Say "Thank you" before hanging up the phone. When children call a friend, they should say, "May I talk to Sandy, please?"
2. Using toy telephones, let the children role-play the best way to call someone or answer a phone call.
3. Let some of the children role-play conversations that aren't polite: "Get Joe on the phone," or "I want to talk to Sandy," or "Let me talk to Eric."
4. Encourage the children to comment on the situations and why they are, or aren't, polite.
5. Using patterns on pages 64 and 67, cut out and color the figures, phones, and phone cords. Using the pattern for hands on page 67, cut out and color the hands.
6. Glue or tape phones to faces and add hands.
7. Cut out cartoon "balloons" for conversations and print words with the marker.

READ A BOOK— ADD A TURKEY FEATHER

MATERIALS AND SUPPLIES

- black cloth background
- orange border
- orange letters
- 10˝ pie pan or plate
- red, brown, orange, and yellow construction paper
- one sheet of white paper
- straight pins (optional)

- wide-tipped black marker
- thumb tacks (optional)
- staples (optional)
- transparent tape
- crayons
- scissors
- glue

INSTRUCTIONS

1. Develop in children a love for books by reading a short book, a story in a book, or a chapter of a book at the same time each day.
2. Using a 10˝ pie pan or dinner plate as a pattern, cut one circle from brown paper for the turkey's body.
3. Use the pattern on page 87 and cut from colored paper as many large red, yellow, orange, and brown tail feathers as desired.
4. Glue a tail feather in place at each side of the turkey. Place the turkey on the bulletin board and put thumbtacks or staples at each side next to the feathers.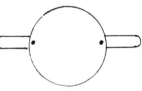
5. Make a book from a piece of white paper 5˝ by 7˝. Fold it in half widthwise and then open it.
6. Make six small wing feathers from the pattern on page 87. Cut red, orange, yellow, or brown feathers. Glue the hand feathers, three on each side, to the turkey's body, with the open book glued to the hand feathers.
7. Using the pattern on page 87, cut head and legs from red paper. Make black eyes and a yellow beak. Make shoes any desired color. Glue head, legs, and shoes in place.
8. Whenever children read a book, they put their name and the book title on a feather. Carefully insert each feather behind the top of the body, between the two glued feathers. If the feathers need to be secured, tape or staple them.

MATERIALS AND SUPPLIES

- dark-green cloth background
- white border
- white letters
- five computer sheets
- thumbtack
- wide-tipped black marker

- any white paper that crayons can write on
  (Used computer paper, clean on one side, is OK.)
- transparent tape
- crayons
- scissors

INSTRUCTIONS

1. Ask the children if they know when and why our baby teeth come out. Teeth facts: At about six or seven years of age, the roots of the baby teeth dissolve gradually and the teeth fall out. The permanent teeth grow in to fill each space left by the baby teeth.
2. Encourage brushing teeth, drinking milk, and eating good food so permanent teeth stay healthy.
3. Using the patterns on page 65, color and cut out the faces. On page 65, cut out the mouths with missing teeth. Attach the mouths to the faces with a small piece of tape.
4. Make one large tooth from the pattern on page 99. Use black marker to outline the tooth. Glue the tooth on a sheet of paper, and with the marker, write the words *crown* and *roots* around the tooth.
5. Write these sentences on the computer sheets:
   Roots of baby teeth dissolve.
   Baby teeth fall out.
   Permanent teeth grow in.
   Teeth have crowns and roots.
6. Use narrow white paper strips above and below the tooth picture. Secure the two glued paper strips with a thumbtack at the top. Glue the ends behind the tooth picture. Glue another paper strip at the back of the tooth picture and continue the strip to the border at the bottom of the bulletin board.

MATERIALS AND SUPPLIES

- dark-blue cloth background
- white border
- white letters
- crayons
- any computer paper that crayons can write on (Used computer paper, clean on one side, is OK.)
- wide-tipped red marker
- scissors

INSTRUCTIONS

1. Ask the children why their parents vote. Possible reasons:
   - to elect a new president for our country every four years
   - to elect a mayor for our town and other offices
   - to elect people who go to our state capitol to work for our state
   - to elect people who go to Washington, D.C., to work for each of our states
2. In the United States, we are allowed to vote for our leaders.
3. We have two main political parties—Republicans and Democrats.
4. The Democratic party's symbol is a donkey.
5. The Republican party's symbol is an elephant.
6. We need to learn about each candidate before we vote for him or her.
7. Newspapers and television give us information to help us make choices.
8. We go to a voting place to vote. (Explain to the children what people do in a voting place.)
9. Using the patterns on page 75, make a gray elephant and a brown donkey. Color them heavily and cut them out. Color and cut the voting booths and people from patterns on page 90.
10. Glue enough computer sheets together to write these four phrases underneath the pictures, using the red marker:
    to elect a president; to elect other leaders; to decide new laws; to decide how leaders should spend our tax money.

MATERIALS AND SUPPLIES

- brown cloth background
- orange border
- orange letters
- crayons

- any white paper that crayons can write on
  (Used computer paper, clean on one side, is OK.)
- wide-tipped black marker
- scissors

INSTRUCTIONS

1. Talk about beginning sounds.
2. Prepare pairs of figures (number optional) from patterns:
   banana and bird, pp. 103, 73; cat and cookie, pp. 70, 85; duck and cake, pp. 90, 61; fish and leaf, pp. 106, 111; gum and cupcake, pp. 86, 95; ham and heart, pp. 63, 98; jacket and cup, pp. 62, 74; lamp and lemon, pp. 63, 103; marbles and milk, pp. 78, 81; nut (walnut) and potato, pp. 112, 109; pumpkin and pear, pp. 106, 103; question mark and hand on mouth (for quiet), p. 99; raindrops and raincoat/hat, pp. 115, 67 and 94; sun and sack, pp. 61, 107; toothbrush and tomato, pp. 58, 93; tent and voting, pp. 112, 90.
3. Color as desired.
4. Additional pairs to use if desired:
   boy's face and butterfly, pp. 62, 108; can and candle, p. 107; donkey and dog, pp. 75, 91; fence and ferris wheel, pp. 84, 97; girl and gumdrops, pp. 90, 74; house and hand, pp. 84, 89; jumping rope and jar, pp. 92, 85; lady and lettuce, pp. 95, 93; moon and mop, pp. 107, 115; nut (walnut) and nail, pp. 112, 59; pan and pencil, pp. 66, 73; quill and queen/crown, pp. 75, 95, 109; robot and raccoon, pp. 74, 111; six and seat belt, pp. 62, 110; teeth in mouth and telephone, pp. 66, 64; volleyball and vegetables, pp. 79, 93; wagon and witch, p. 107; yogurt and yarn, pp. 81, 107; zipper and zero, pp. 88, 95.

MATERIALS AND SUPPLIES

- medium-blue cloth background
- black border
- black letters
- crayons

- any white paper that crayons can write on
  (Used computer paper, clean on one side, is OK.)
- scissors

INSTRUCTIONS

1. Ask the children to tell about things that make them angry.
2. Let the children role-play these situations.
3. Discuss ways they can solve their anger problems.
4. Ask the children to draw themselves in angry situations. Display the pictures.
5. Use five face patterns from pages 64 to 67. Color and cut them out. Lightly tape to each face:
   a turned-down mouth, p. 65; angry eyebrows, p. 65
6. After the bulletin board is up for a few days, replace it with a bulletin board titled "What Makes Me Happy?" Remove the angry mouths and eyebrows from each face.

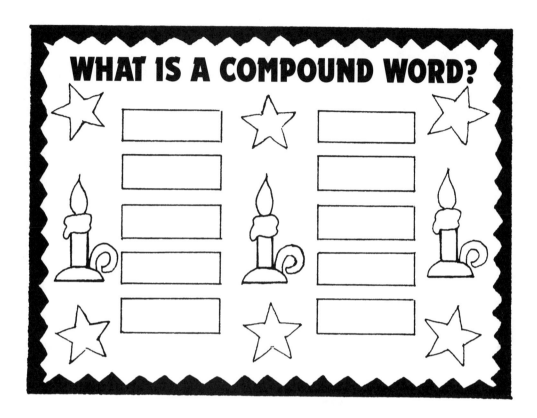

MATERIALS AND SUPPLIES

- black cloth background
- red border
- red letters
- crayons
- white computer paper, amount optional
  (Used computer paper, clean on one side, is OK.)
- wide-tipped red marker
- scissors

INSTRUCTIONS

1. Discuss with children what a compound word is: a word that is made up of two or more words that are words themselves.
2. Prepare words for the bulletin board, number optional. Cut computer sheets in half lengthwise. Write one compound word on each half sheet. Use a wide-tipped red marker.
3. Make stars and candles from the patterns on page 109. Use yellow for stars, and color candles red with yellow flames and white holders. Color heavily and then cut out the items. Arrange them on the bulletin board and around the room.

MATERIALS AND SUPPLIES

- red cloth background
- white border
- white letters
- crayons
- scissors

- any white paper that crayons can write on (Used computer paper, clean on one side, is OK.)
- transparent tape

INSTRUCTIONS

1. Use any patterns on pages 64 to 67 to make four faces. Color as desired and cut out.
2. Cut two left tongues and two right tongues from the patterns on page 65. Color them pink and cut them out. Tape them lightly in place with a small piece of tape so they can be removed and the faces used for other bulletin boards.
3. Make the pie and two cakes from the patterns on pages 71 and 72. Color and cut them out.
4. Discuss cutting desserts into equal parts. Ask the children if they know how much dessert each child will get to eat.
5. Let the children draw pictures of other things such as twelve cupcakes in a pan, sandwiches on a tray, slices of meat on a plate, cups of milk, or eggs in a frying pan, and divide them equally among the four children pictured on the bulletin board.

SOME TREES STAY GREEN: WHY?

MATERIALS AND SUPPLIES

- medium-blue cloth background
- black border
- black letters
- black, yellow, and green colored paper (Several shades of green are preferable so the trees will stand out individually.)
- large brown grocery bag (optional)
- newspapers (optional)

- any white paper that crayons can write on (Used computer paper, clean on one side, is OK.)
- black, yellow, and green paints (optional)
- wide-tipped black marker
- wide, clear shipping tape
- a 6″ saucer or a 10″ plate
- crayons
- glue

INSTRUCTIONS

1. Ask the children if there are trees that don't change colors or lose their leaves in autumn. Evergreen trees have dark-green needlelike leaves and stay green all winter. In the spring new, light-green needlelike leaves begin to appear at the end of each dark-green cluster of leaves. So the leaves are always green.
2. Cut black tree trunks from the pattern on page 68 (number optional).
3. Using the pattern for tree crowns on page 68, fold paper and cut two kinds of crowns. One has straight lines and the other, from the optional dotted-line pattern, has pointed sides. If you use white paper for crowns, color the crowns different shades of green—light to very dark—for variation. As an option, cut crowns from colored paper, brown grocery bags, or newspapers, and make them different shades of green.
4. Glue trunks in place.
5. Outline each tree with black marker, if needed, so it stands out from the others.
6. Cut a yellow sun by tracing around a 6″ saucer or a larger plate.
7. To make a very large tree crown for the wall of your classroom, cut open six large brown grocery bags down the back seams and cut off the bottoms. Open the bags and glue the six bags together, overlapping each 1/2″.
8. Cut a triangular crown from the top center down to each corner. The tree crown will be 6′ tall and 4′ wide at the bottom. Paint it green.
9. Cut a trunk 6″ wide and 16″ long. Paint it black. Glue the trunk to the bottom of the tree, overlapping 1/2″.
10. Tape the tree to the wall with the wide tape.

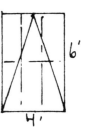

MATERIALS AND SUPPLIES

- dark-blue cloth background
- white border
- white letters
- colored paper (optional)
- glue

- any white paper that crayons can write on
  (Used computer paper, clean on one side, is OK.)
- crayons
- scissors

INSTRUCTIONS

1. Discuss syllables. (Hold your finger under your chin. For every syllable in a word, your chin goes down, if the word is pronounced correctly.)
2. Prepare these bulletin board patterns:
   pencil, p. 73; strawberry, p. 93; lemon, p. 103; watermelon, p. 103; turkey, p. 86; candle, p. 109; telephone, p. 64; cantaloupe, p. 110; star, p. 109; squirrel, p. 88; raccoon, p. 111; cheese, p. 81; raspberry, p. 103; refrigerator, p. 114; banana, p. 103; television, p. 60
3. Color as desired.

MONEY: WHAT IS IT FOR?

MATERIALS AND SUPPLIES
- black cloth background
- green border
- green letters
- green, brown, and gray paper (optional)
- black felt-tipped pen
- any white paper that crayons can write on
  (Used computer paper, clean on one side, is OK.)
- crayons
- scissors

INSTRUCTIONS
1. Show the children a dollar bill, half dollar, quarter, dime, nickel, and penny. Ask them if they know what each one is.
2. Pass them around and let each child hold them, one at a time.
3. Discuss the size, color, and value of each.
4. Ask the children what money is used for: to pay for houses, rent, cars, food, clothes, doctors, dentists, stoves, refrigerators, haircuts, and so on.
5. Point out that we have to earn money in order to purchase things we need to live. We should never spend more money than we earn.
6. Make money samples from patterns on page 100. Put them on the bulletin board: green dollar; gray half dollar, quarter, dime, and nickel; brown penny.
7. Prepare bulletin board items and color as desired.
   cap, p. 77; jacket, p. 62; refrigerator, p. 114; ham, p. 63; towel, p. 58; shoe, p. 116; carrots, p. 58; bread, p. 63; toothbrush, p. 58; car, p. 114; house, p. 84; lamp, p. 63; television, p. 60; cup, p. 74; saucer, p. 110; glasses, p. 60
8. Ask the children to bring newspaper ads with pictures of things to buy and the cost of each. Discuss them. Show how many dollars it takes for these things.
9. Put the newspaper advertisements and costs around the outside or on the bulletin board.

WHAT IS A THERMOMETER?

MATERIALS AND SUPPLIES

- dark-blue cloth background
- white border
- white letters
- wide-tipped black marker
- transparent tape
- red paper (optional)
- any white paper that crayons can write on
  (Used computer paper, clean on one side, is OK.)
- crayons
- scissors
- glue

INSTRUCTIONS

1. Talk about thermometers and what they are used for: to measure air temperatures inside and outside, to tell when meat is done or when candy reaches certain temperatures, to measure body temperatures, to tell how hot the water is in a swimming pool, and so on.

2. Heat causes the mercury in the thermometer tube to rise higher.

3. Ask the children how they feel when the temperature outside is high and the air is hot. How do they feel when it is very cold and the temperature is low?

4. What time of the year is hot? cold? not too hot or too cold?

5. To make a thermometer, glue enough white papers together for a strip 48″ long and 7″ wide. With a black marker, make two long black lines, 1″ apart, from the top, continuing down the center to within 1 1/2″ of the bottom. Glue a 5″ round circle of red paper, or white paper colored bright red, at the bottom of the thermometer, still leaving 1 1/2″ below. Beginning at the red ball, draw black temperature lines across the thermometer every 3″ until you reach the top. The bottom line can be –20°; the next one –10°; and so on. Continue by 10s until you reach 110° F at the top.

6. For the mercury tube, cut a red strip of paper 1″ wide and 6″ long, or any desired length. Attach the bottom of the strip to the red ball.

7. Fold the top of the red strip at the place where the predicted temperature is for the day, adding additional red strips as needed.

8. To cut icicles, fold used computer paper in half lengthwise. Draw a short icicle about 4″ long, one about 7″ long, and a third 4″ long. (Do not cut the folded side apart entirely.)

9. Use face patterns from pages 64, 65, 66, and 101 (trace the face on page 101 and reverse it). Make four mittens from the pattern on page 71. Make button mouths, with the space around them, for the two side figures from the pattern on page 59 and tape them on lightly. Earmuffs and scarf patterns are on page 72. The hat pattern is on page 92. Tape the caps on lightly. Eyes looking down are on page 101. The serious mouth for the boy with the scarf is on page 71. Tape it to his face lightly.

10. The children can report to the class temperature readings in other parts of the country or the world.

MATERIALS AND SUPPLIES

- dark-blue cloth background
- yellow border
- yellow letters
- brown, red, yellow, and white paper
- brown grocery bag (optional)
- cotton or cotton balls (optional)
- transparent tape

- any white paper that crayons can write on
  (Used computer paper, clean on one side, is OK.)
- paints (optional)
- crayons
- scissors
- glue

INSTRUCTIONS

1. Talk about snow. Read a snow story such as *A Snowy Day* by Ezra Keats.
2. Ask the children if they know where snow comes from. Water droplets (vapor) high in the air form ice crystals of different shapes that fall to the ground as snow.
3. Prepare a snow strip as wide as the bulletin board and approximately 8″, or more, deep. Use white paper, cotton, or grocery bags painted white.
4. Cut a barn from the pattern on page 84. Use red paper with black windows; use white paper and color it dark red and black; or use a grocery bag painted red with black windows. Add white paper or cotton or a grocery bag painted white for snow on the barn roof.
5. Make a yellow house from the pattern on page 84. Cut black windows and a red door and roof from colored papers, or use white paper colored heavily or a painted grocery bag. Add paper or cotton snow.
6. From the pattern on page 85, cut a brown tree trunk and branches; use white paper and color it brown; or use a grocery bag and brown paint. Add paper or cotton snow.
7. Using the pattern on page 84, cut a fence from red paper, white paper colored red, or a grocery bag painted red. Add paper or cotton snow.
8. Cut snowflakes from white paper using the snowflake pattern on page 84, or use cotton balls.

MATERIALS AND SUPPLIES

- light-blue cloth background
- red border
- red letters
- red, orange, and black paper
- 3 sheets of white computer paper
- wide-tipped black marker
- crayons
- scissors

INSTRUCTIONS

1. Prepare the red cardinal from the pattern on page 92. Use red paper. Color an orange beak, a black eye with orange around it, a black face, black boots, an orange scarf and earmuffs, and a black head-band. Outline wing with black pen.
2. Read about birds. They keep cool in summer and warm in winter. Birds are warm-blooded. Eating more food in winter helps them keep warm. Fluffing their feathers also keeps them warm in winter. In summer they flatten their feathers to keep cool.
3. We can help birds in winter by regularly feeding them sunflower seeds and birdseed. Supply fresh water and tiny gravel stones to help them digest their food.
4. Let the children color birds from the pattern on page 92, or draw their own.
5. Use three sheets of computer paper and write these labels: warm-blooded, fluff feathers for warmth, eat more in winter for warmth. Use a wide-tipped marker for making letters and a black border around each paper.

WHAT IS EXERCISE?

MATERIALS AND SUPPLIES
- dark-green cloth background
- white border
- white letters
- colored paper (optional)
- wide-tipped black marker (optional)
- world map (optional)
- any white paper that crayons can write on
  (Used computer paper, clean on one side, is OK.)
- transparent tape
- wide, clear shipping tape
- scissors
- crayons

INSTRUCTIONS
1. Discuss the word *exercise* with the children. See how many types of exercises they can name. List them on the chalkboard: in-line skating, jumping rope, hopscotch, baseball, basketball, football, bicycling, swimming, aerobics, walking, water-skiing, jumping, running, ballet, and so on.
2. Exercise is important for people of all ages. Discuss the reasons for exercising: to keep your heart and body healthy, to live longer, to have fewer health problems.
3. We exercise from birth, moving arms and legs.
4. Give each child a sheet of paper and let them draw themselves doing one of the exercises listed on the chalkboard.
5. Using the patterns on pages 76, 77, 104, and 111, color the Danny Dibby figures, in-line skates, and water as desired, or use colored paper. Cut them out, tape parts together, and place them on the bulletin board. Tape the children's drawings around the wall.
6. Outline the figures and pictures with marker if needed.
7. If this is a year for summer or winter Olympics, discuss them with the children. Explain that they are contests. Those who enter work hard and train for four or more years. Often new records are set. Ask the children what kinds of exercises people compete in: skating, swimming, diving, running, jumping, pole-vaulting, gymnastics, tobogganing, shot-put, skiing, hockey, basketball, track, relay, weight lifting, and so on.
8. There are Olympics for children, Special Olympics for persons with disabilities, and Senior Olympics for older people.
9. Encourage the children to bring pictures of people who enter the Olympics.
10. List the people and in what events they compete.
11. Find the towns and countries of the participants on a map and place dots there. Try to determine how many miles they travel to get to the Olympics. Show on the map where the next Olympics will be held and in what year.

BIRDS FOR BOOKS

MATERIALS AND SUPPLIES

- black letters
- black paper
- colored paper
- brown grocery bags (optional)
- paints (optional)
- cotton balls (optional)

- any white paper that crayons can write on
  (Used computer paper, clean on one side, is OK.)
- wide, clear shipping tape
- crayons
- transparent tape

INSTRUCTIONS

1. Using the bird pattern on page 68, cut as many birds as desired. Use white paper and color the cutouts, or use colored paper. Put the birds in a box on the table.
2. Encourage the children to read library books by adding birds to a tree for each book read. Have children write their name on the back of the bird and the book title on the front when they finish a book.
3. Assemble the large tree from the October directions on page 16. Cut out the tree from black paper, or use grocery bags and black paint. Tape it to the wall with wide, clear shipping tape.
4. From the pattern on page 84, cut snowflakes from white paper, or else use cotton balls. Tape them to the wall.
5. Tape the birds to limbs and smaller branches.

WINTER: WHERE DOES FOOD COME FROM?

MATERIALS AND SUPPLIES
- dark-green cloth background
- light-green border
- light-green letters
- white computer paper
- colored paper (optional)
- wide-tipped black marker
- any white paper that crayons can write on
  (Used computer paper, clean on one side, is OK.)
- crayons
- scissors
- glue

INSTRUCTIONS
1. If you live where it is too cold to grow winter fruits and vegetables, ask the children where most of these things come from in winter: tomatoes, green beans, corn, carrots, lettuce, lemons, oranges, grapefruit, strawberries, potatoes, and so on.
2. On a large map of the United States, point to the place where you live. Point also to the states of Florida, California, Arizona, Hawaii, and Texas. Explain that winter vegetables and fruits come from those states. Ask if anyone has visited these states.
3. Ask the children why these things grow in winter in those states. They are warm in the winter or have a warm region in their southern part, which is closest to the equator. (Explain that the equator area is the warmest part of the Earth.)
4. If you live in the warmest parts of these southern states, you can ask and expand on the same questions. Many children have never experienced cold and snow. Perhaps they don't know their areas provide food for people in the North, where it is cold in the winter. Show pictures of snow.
5. Using the fruit and vegetable patterns on pages 92, 93, 103, and 109, color heavily and cut out these foods, one or more of each:
   red tomatoes and red strawberries, p. 93; yellow corn and brown potatoes, p. 109; green beans and green lettuce, p. 93; oranges and yellow grapefruit, p. 93; yellow lemons, p. 103; orange carrots, p. 58 or 92
6. Put white paper behind each, a little larger than the fruits and vegetables, so they show up well.
7. Make five labels from two sheets of computer paper cut into fourths widthwise. Using black marker, print the names of the five states where winter fruits and vegetables grow.
8. Using the palm-tree patterns on pages 78 and 108, make green leaves and a brown trunk. Reverse one tree so the two trees are leaning toward each other. Glue parts together.

MATERIALS AND SUPPLIES

- red cloth background
- white border
- white letters
- a child's book of George Washington to read to the children (for example, the picture book *George Washington: Father of Our Country* by David Adler)
- any white paper that crayons can write on (Used computer paper, clean on one side, is OK.)
- wide-tipped black marker
- crayons
- scissors
- glue

INSTRUCTIONS

1. From patterns on pages 67, 88, 89, and 101, prepare the figures of George Washington and a boy talking to him, asking him questions. For the boy's face, reverse the pattern and add the arm on page 67. Color heavily as desired and glue arms to the figures.
2. Outline the figures in marker, if needed.
3. Prepare the "balloon" from white paper. Print the words: "Hello, Mr. Washington. May I please ask you a question?"
4. Tell the children that you are going to read them the story of George Washington's life. Ask them to listen carefully, because when you are finished reading, you will choose someone to be Mr. Washington. Then the boys and girls will ask the chosen person a question about things they heard in the story. "Mr. Washington" will try to answer questions as if he or she really were George Washington. Remind children to address the person playing Mr. Washington with respect by saying "Mr. Washington, may I please ask you a question?" Choose as many children to act the part of Mr. Washington as you desire. Each "Mr. Washington" could answer three or four questions before you choose another child to play Mr. Washington. Continue as long as interest is sustained.

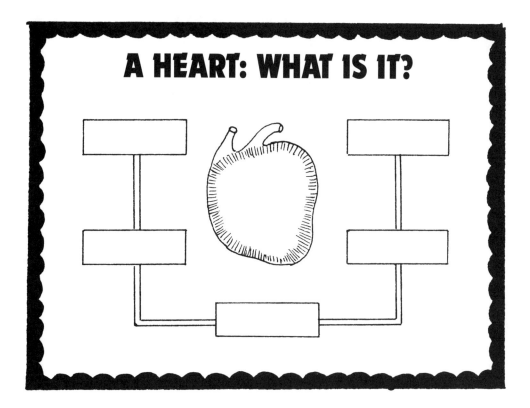

MATERIALS AND SUPPLIES

- red cloth background
- pink border
- black letters
- pink paper
- 5 sheets of white computer paper

- crayons
- scissors
- glue
- wide-tipped red marker

INSTRUCTIONS

1. Discuss the heart with children. Before birth, when you were only 1″ long, your heart was beating. The heart is a pump. The heart sends blood through tubes called veins and arteries. (Look at your hands and arms for blood vessels.) The heart sends oxygen and food to the body cells. The heart is located in the center of your chest. There are two pumps coming from the heart. About 2¹/2 quarts of blood are pumped through a child's heart every minute. In one year a child's heart pumps nearly 1,000 gallons of blood. People's hearts are about the size of their fist. Healthy foods help your heart stay well.
2. Cut five sheets of computer paper in half lengthwise for labels. With the marker, write these words for labels: pump, beating, veins, arteries, oxygen, chest, fist, healthy foods, 2¹/2 quarts, 1,000 gallons.
3. Foods low in fat help our hearts stay healthy. Vegetables, chicken, fish, fruits, whole-grain breads and cereals, and skim milk help your heart stay well.
4. Cut a heart from the pattern on page 68. Color it darker pink around the edge and white in the center. Outline it with black marker.
5. Connect the labels with pink paper strips 1″ wide.

WHAT IS A RAIN FOREST?

MATERIALS AND SUPPLIES

- medium-blue cloth background
- black border
- black letters
- colored paper (optional)
- crayons with as many shades
  of green as possible

- any white paper that crayons can write on
  (Used computer paper, clean on one side, is OK.)
- transparent tape
- scissors
- glue

INSTRUCTIONS

1. Ask the children if they know what a rain forest is.
2. What does the word rain tell us about this kind of forest?
3. A rain forest has warm weather all year and lots of rain.
4. Get a children's book about rain forests from the library. Two good books are *The Great Kapok Tree* by Lynne Cherry and *Tropical Rainforests* by Gail Gibbons. Read the chosen book to the children and show them the pictures.
5. Rain forests have very tall trees. Many grow to be 250′ high. (To illustrate this, draw a 1″ high orange tree on the chalkboard, representing a 10′ high orange tree. Twenty-five inches above the top of your orange tree is where a rain forest tree would stand in comparison. This is as tall as a 25-story sky-scraper.) These tall trees are the upper canopy of the forest.
6. Smaller trees, such as orange, banana, and palm trees, form the lower canopy of trees, along with the vines and plants. Very little light reaches the floor of the rain forest.
7. Most rain forests are located near the equator. Point to the equator on a map. That is the warmest part of the world.
8. Many animals live in rain forests: bats, alligators, sloths, flying squirrels, parrots, sunbirds, toucans, hummingbirds, golden frogs, lizards, snakes, deer, antelope, butterflies, spider monkeys, and so on.
9. Make these animals from patterns: tan flying squirrel, page 88 (using the dotted lines); green snakes with black scales, p. 69; yellow frog, brightly colored butterflies, and toucans, page 108 (black bodies, yellow beaks and faces, orange around the blue eyes, blue legs, patch of red underneath where the tail meets the body, and brown twig).
10. Make trees and plants from patterns and color them various shades of green for contrast: dark-green orange tree (follow dotted lines), orange fruit, and brown trunk, p. 72; green banana leaves, p. 102 (four for each tree), and green trunk, p. 72; palm leaves, p. 108, and trunk, p. 78; brown vine, p. 95; green plant leaf, p. 100 (follow dotted lines); dark-green snake plant with leaves edged in yellow, p. 108; green Christmas cactus, p. 108; rain-forest leaf, p. 102; green plant leaf, p. 111 (follow dotted lines)
11. Let the children draw and color rain-forest animals or color the patterns of the animals. Tape the animals around the outside of the bulletin board.

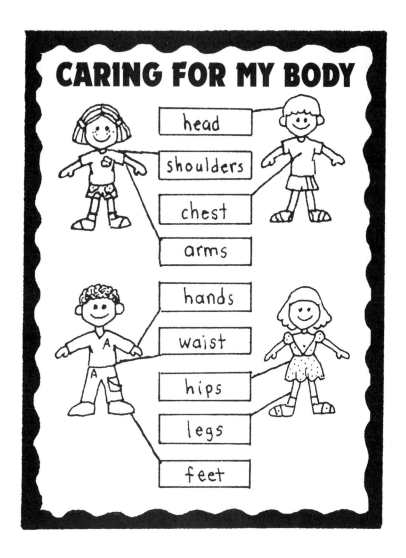

MATERIALS AND SUPPLIES

- black cloth background
- white border
- white letters
- paper strips or bias tape (optional)
- 9 sheets of computer paper
- pins

- any white paper that crayons can write on
  (Used computer paper, clean on one side, is OK.)
- wide-tipped black marker
- crayons
- scissors
- glue

INSTRUCTIONS

1. Cut out figures of two girls and two boys from any patterns on pages 58 to 63. Color heavily.
2. Make ten labels from five sheets of paper cut in half lengthwise. Print the name of a body part on each: head, neck, shoulders, chest, arms, hands, waist, hips, legs, feet.
3. Cut white paper or bias-tape strips to go from the labels to body parts. Attach them with pins.
4. Discuss care of the body: bathing, washing hair, combing hair, brushing teeth, cutting fingernails and toenails when needed, washing hands before eating, wearing clean clothes, wearing shoes that aren't too tight, eating healthy foods, exercising, and so on.

MATERIALS AND SUPPLIES

- black cloth background
- white border
- white letters
- crayons

- any white paper that crayons can write on
  (Used computer paper, clean on one side, is OK.)
- newspaper advertisements for food
- scissors

INSTRUCTIONS

1. Prepare these foods from patterns and color heavily:
   pink ham, p. 63; chocolate cupcake, p. 95; purple grapes, p. 110; orange carrots, p. 58; green peppers, p. 83; brown cookie, p. 85; brown bread, p. 63; blue fish, p. 106; yellow cheese, p. 81; brown potato, p. 109; white milk, p. 81; red tomato and red strawberry, p. 93; red apple, p. 62
   Place white irregular-shape papers behind each.
2. Ask the children to bring in pictures of foods with prices from the grocery ads in the newspapers, or ads from grocery stores.
3. Display the pictures in the grocery ads and discuss the possible cost of a meal for a family.
4. Discuss the foods that cost the most money and discuss foods that are not so expensive. Talk about the cost of foods that are good for you.
5. Ask the children what foods they like best.

WHAT IS WEATHER?

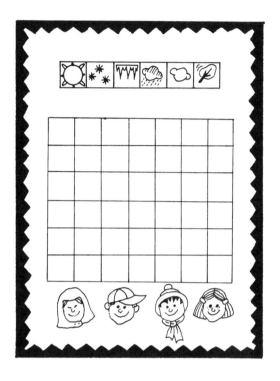

MATERIALS AND SUPPLIES

- medium-blue cloth background
- black border
- black letters
- 6 sheets of white computer paper
  (for the calendar)
- wide-tipped black marker
- black felt-tip pen
- black paper
- any white paper that crayons can write on
  (Used computer paper, clean on one side, is OK.)
- transparent tape
- crayons
- scissors
- glue
- yardstick
- pencil

INSTRUCTIONS

1. To make a calendar with 3″ squares for a month, place six computer sheets together (three above and three below), without overlapping. Tape the adjoining edges together.
2. Turn the taped paper over so the taped sides are on the back.
3. With a yardstick and pencil, begin at the left side and mark off every 3″ across the top and bottom. Connect the dots from top to bottom with the felt-tipped pen. (There will be leftover paper at the right.)
4. Starting at the top, mark off every 3″ down both sides. Connect the dots. (There will be leftover paper.)
5. Count off seven rows at the top. Cut off the extra paper.
6. Count down six rows on the sides. Cut off the extra paper. You now have a calendar with seven rows across for seven days, and six rows down for six weeks. (Some months require six rows when the first day is on a Friday or Saturday and there are 31 days.)
7. With the wide marker, print the dates in the proper places for March.
8. Choose and color four faces only, from patterns on pages 58 to 63. To represent four kinds of weather, add a cap, page 60; a rain coat and hat, pages 67 and 94; and a scarf and wool hat, page 94. The fourth figure represents warm, sunny weather (no hat). Color and tape the figures in place.
9. Prepare weather symbols from the patterns on page 94. Color the sun yellow with orange points. Color the upper part of the rain cloud dark blue. Color the tree in the wind as desired.
10. Cut out the letters for the word *March*, or print them on white paper. Place them above the calendar.
11. Ask the children what they think weather is. It is what is happening in the air around us. It changes from day to day.
12. Ask the children how many of their parents watch the weather report on TV or listen to it on the radio.
13. Let the boys and girls tell you what time of the year the symbols represent. Also, ask what time of the year they like best and why.
14. Ask the children to check the newspaper or television for the next day's weather report daily for one month. Tape the predicted weather symbol on the bulletin board calendar. See how many predictions come true. Continue for every day of March.

MATERIALS AND SUPPLIES

- medium-blue cloth background
- green border
- green letters
- crayons

- any white paper that crayons can write on
  (Used computer paper, clean on one side, is OK.)
- scissors

INSTRUCTIONS

1. Make a cow from the pattern on page 82. Color it black and white. Give it a pink nose.
2. Make a barn and fence from the patterns on page 84. Color them red.
3. For the grass, use the pattern on page 80. Color it green.
4. From the patterns on page 80, make a truck and dairy. Color the tires black, the cab dark blue. Color the dairy building brown.
5. From the pattern on page 81, make a milk jug. Color the cap green. Make Swiss cheese and color it yellow. Make an ice cream carton and color the lid purple and the letters purple. Make a yogurt cup and color it green. Make a box of butter. Color it yellow. Cut them out.
6. Ask the children where milk comes from. Milk comes from cows. (Many people in the world also get milk from goats, sheep, camels, llamas, reindeer, and water buffaloes.) Milk is an almost perfect food. It is very good for your health. It makes strong bones and teeth. Dairy cows give milk. Most dairy cows are black-and-white Holsteins. They live on farms and eat grass, hay, and corn. Farmers put the milk in tanks to keep it cold. The milk is pumped out of the farmer's tanks and into a tank truck. The truck takes the milk to dairies, where it is put into jugs and delivered to stores.
7. Some milk is made into cheese, yogurt, butter, and ice cream.
8. Let each child draw a cow, color it, and cut it out or else make one from a pattern and color it. A barn and many cows can be a farm scene.

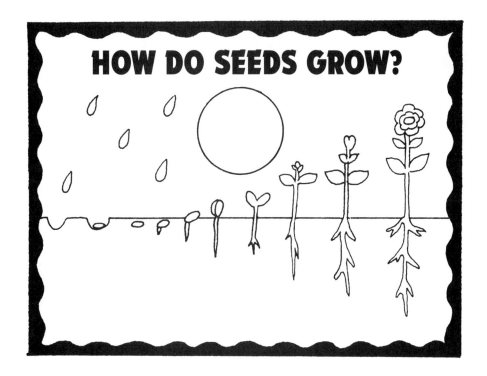

MATERIALS AND SUPPLIES

- medium-blue cloth background
- dark-green border (Outline with black marker, if needed.)
- dark-green letters
- brown grocery bags
- colored paper

- any white paper that crayons can write on (Used computer paper, clean on one side, is O.K.)
- felt-tipped black marker
- crayons
- scissors
- glue

INSTRUCTIONS

1. Make a brown seed and the five stages of seed growth from the patterns on page 99. Color heavily and cut them out.
2. From the patterns on page 81, make a yellow-and-orange flower and black roots. Glue them together at the dotted lines.
3. Make the brown earth from paper bags. Cut the back seam open and cut off the bottom of each bag. Make the earth long enough to reach across your bulletin board and wide enough for the longest flower roots. You may need to glue parts of bags together to make them the right size.
4. Outline each item with black marker, if needed.
5. Use the pattern on page 115 to make white raindrops.
6. Trace around a dinner plate, on yellow paper, to make a sun.
7. Ask the children if they have ever planted seeds. Let them tell about their experiences.
8. Explain the stages of seed growth and what seeds need.
9. If desired, give each child a polystyrene foam cup (with a hole in the bottom for drainage). Add potting soil and let the children plant seeds. (Tomato plants are simple to grow. Take seeds from a healthy tomato and plant them in the soil. Keep them moist, but not too wet and out of direct sunlight for a couple weeks.)

UMBRELLAS AND RAINCOATS IN APRIL: WHY?

MATERIALS AND SUPPLIES
- medium-blue cloth background
- black border
- black letters
- dark-blue paper for clouds (optional)
- wide-tipped black marker
- any white paper that crayons can write on
  (Used computer paper, clean on one side, is OK.)
- transparent tape
- crayons
- glue

INSTRUCTIONS

1. Using the patterns, color and cut out seven figures from pages 58 to 63. Make seven raincoats from page 67, five rain hats from page 94, six boots from page 62, and two umbrellas and handles (three parts) from page 89. Color heavily with bright colors and cut the pieces out. Glue two parts of the umbrella handle together at the dotted line. Glue the handle to the umbrella top at the dotted line. Tape or glue rain hats and coats on the figures. Make white rain drops from the pattern on page 115 and tape them to the bulletin board.
2. Ask the children why umbrellas and raincoats are good to have in April. Teach the rhyme:
   April showers
   Bring May flowers.
3. Umbrellas have been used for many hundreds of years. They used to be made from oiled cloth and wood. In ancient Egypt only rich people were allowed to have them. Rich ladies in England, many years ago, carried silk umbrellas trimmed with pretty lace.
4. Let the children draw and color themselves in raincoats or with umbrellas. As an option, give children a pattern and let them color it brightly. Place the figures on the bulletin board and around the outside.
5. Outline pictures with marker, if needed.

MATERIALS AND SUPPLIES

- medium-blue cloth background
- black border
- black letters
- crayons

- any white paper that crayons can write on
  (Used computer paper, clean on one side, is OK.)
- scissors

INSTRUCTIONS

1. Ask the children to name as many farm animals as they can and tell what each is used for:
   cow—milk (cattle for meat)
   horse—work
   duck—food
   sheep—wool, meat
   chicken—meat, eggs
   pig—meat
   cat—work (catches mice)
   dog—work (guards property, herds sheep)
2. Cut animals from patterns on pages 82, 83, and 90. Color animals and cut them out: black-and-white cow, pink pig, brown horse, white sheep with black face and legs, brown chicken, white duck with orange bill and feet, orange cat.
3. Let the children make farm animals on white paper or color patterns.

MATERIALS AND SUPPLIES

- medium-blue cloth background
- black border
- black letters
- brown grocery bags (optional)
- green paint (optional)
- green, brown, yellow, and red paper (optional)
- transparent tape
- any white paper that crayons can write on (Used computer paper, clean on one side, is OK.)
- encyclopedia pictures of floods, rain, and so on
- crayons
- scissors
- glue

INSTRUCTIONS

1. For grass, use green paper or brown grocery bags painted green. Length and width of grass is optional.
2. Prepare a barn from the pattern on page 84. Color it red or use red paper. Color windows black. From the pattern on page 84, make a yellow house. Color windows and roofs black and the door red, or use colored paper.
3. From the pattern on page 85, cut a bare tree and color it brown, or use brown paper. Cut a tree crown from page 85. Color it green or use colored paper. Glue or tape crown to tree trunk.
4. Cut two red fences from the pattern on page 84. Cut dark-blue clouds and raindrops from page 115, or use white paper and color them dark blue.
5. Add colored flowers from the pattern on page 84.
6. Ask the children which things need water from the rain: gardens, animals, farmers' fields, flowers, grass, trees, people, forests, mountains, lakes, and so on.
7. Ask the children what happens when there is not enough rain: grass and plants turn brown, fish die when rivers dry up, the ground turns to dust, farmers lose their crops, and so on.
8. Raindrops fall from dark clouds. The larger the drops, the faster they fall.
9. Discuss what happens when there is too much rain: floods, good ground washes away, crops and trees wash away, homes are destroyed, and so on. (Show pictures from encyclopedias and books.)

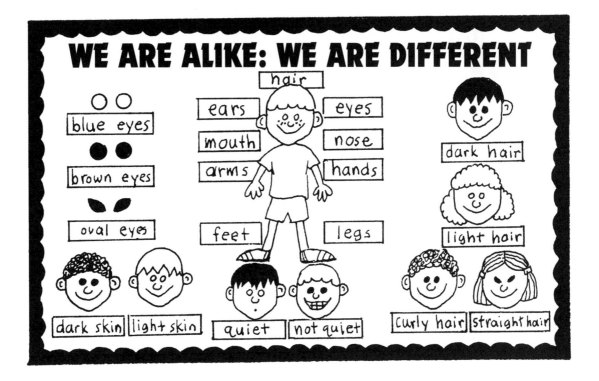

MATERIALS AND SUPPLIES:

- dark-green cloth background
- white border
- white letters
- broad-tipped black marker (optional)
- transparent tape
- pins

- any white paper that crayons can write on
  (Used computer paper, clean on one side, is OK.)
- crayons
- scissors
- glue

INSTRUCTIONS:

1. Discuss ways in which we are all alike and ways we are different, but point out that each of us is special.
2. Make one full-length body from the pattern on page 116 and one face from a pattern on page 65. Glue or tape the face to the body at the dotted line (skin color optional). Color the clothes and the shoes. Cut out the shoes along the dotted lines. Fit the ankles into the tops of the shoes. Glue them so the dotted lines do not show.
3. Cut three pairs of eyes from patterns on page 66. Color one round pair blue, one round pair brown, and the oval pair brown.
4. Make four faces from the patterns on pages 64, 65, and 66. Color one girl's hair yellow, one boy's hair brown, one girl's hair straight and dark, one boy's hair curly and black.
5. Cut two faces from the patterns on pages 64 and 66. Color one boy's skin light, the other dark.
6. Cut two faces from the patterns on pages 65 and 67. Add a toothy smile from the mouth pattern on page 66 and tape it lightly to one face. Add a button mouth from the pattern on page 59. Tape it lightly to the face of the dark-haired boy.
7. Cut each of the five sheets of computer paper into four parts widthwise for labels. Print words on labels with black marker. (See bulletin board picture for words.)
8. Tape or pin parts on the bulletin board.

MATERIALS AND SUPPLIES

- medium-blue cloth background
- dark-green border
- dark-green letters
- brown grocery bags (for soil)
- 6 sheets of computer paper
  cut in half, lengthwise

- any white paper that crayons can write on
  (Used computer paper, clean on one side, is OK.)
- black felt-tipped pen
- scissors
- glue

INSTRUCTIONS

1. There are many tiny parts to these items, so you can cut them out and leave a white border around each, if desired. Color each item heavily.
2. Use the pattern on page 92 and color the carrot orange. Stems, roots, and leaves are green.
3. Make a potato plant using the pattern on page 94. Color stems and leaves green and potatoes and roots brown.
4. Use the radish pattern on page 96. Color the radish red, stems and leaves green, and roots brown.
5. The turnip pattern is on page 93. Color the top of the turnip purple, the bottom white. Leaves and stems are green. Roots are brown.
6. The red beet pattern is on page 96. Color the beet dark red, the leaves green and red, the stems red, and the roots brown.
7. The pepper plant is on page 95. Color the pepper red. (When green peppers are left on the vine, they eventually turn red and are much sweeter.) Color the stems and leaves green, and the roots brown.
8. Use the green bean plant pattern on page 98. Color the beans, stems, and leaves green, and the roots brown.
9. Use the lettuce pattern and roots on page 93. Color the lettuce pale green and the roots brown, and glue the roots to the bottom of the lettuce at the dotted line. Outline the vegetable and underground roots with black marker.
10. Make a tomato plant from the pattern on page 97. Color the tomatoes red, the stems and leaves green, and the roots brown.
11. If desired, outline all the vegetables, leaves, stems, and roots with black marker.
12. Using one or more large brown grocery bags, make a strip of soil as deep as desired.
13. Cut a yellow sun by tracing around a saucer or plate.
14. Ask the children to name as many vegetables as they can. Write them on the chalkboard. Ask if the vegetables grow above or below ground. Stress the importance of eating vegetables daily for good health. Let the children tell you what their mothers make from vegetables: mashed or baked potatoes, salads, mixed vegetables, vegetable casseroles, soups, and so on.
15. Let the children color vegetable patterns or draw their own vegetables.
16. Put a name label under each vegetable on the bulletin board, if desired.

INSECTS: WHAT ARE THEY?

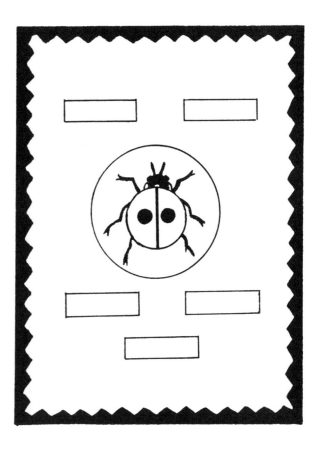

MATERIALS AND SUPPLIES
- yellow cloth background
- red border
- red letters
- encyclopedia and books showing pictures of insects
- one dinner plate
- black, red, and yellow paper (optional)
- any white paper that crayons can write on (Used computer paper, clean on one side, is OK.)
- computer paper
- wide-tipped black marker
- crayons
- scissors
- glue

INSTRUCTIONS
1. Make a ladybug from the pattern on page 98. Use colored paper or white paper and color it heavily: red wings with two black spots. Make a black back stripe, black legs, black eyes, a black head, and black antennae. Make three yellow spots on two sides and the back of the head. Cut out the bug. Outline the two yellow spots on the side of the head with black marker.
2. Using yellow paper, trace around a dinner plate with wide black marker. Cut out the circle, including the black border, and place it behind the ladybug.
3. Show the children pictures of insects. Use the encyclopedia or read a children's book about insects, such as *Amazing Insects* by L. A. Mound or *Bug Wise* by Pamela Hickman.
4. Discuss insects. They are often small, with three pairs of legs, a segmented body (three parts), and usually two pairs of wings and two antennae.
5. Insects include the bee, ant, cockroach, termite, mosquito, cricket, wasp, ladybug, moth, dragonfly, flea, butterfly, firefly, walking stick, louse, and fly.
6. Insects live nearly everywhere on earth. You find them from snowy places to deserts.
7. Some insects make noises. Some insects get air (or breathe) through holes in their sides.
8. Some insects bite animals and people.
9. Insects are many colors.
10. Insects are food for birds, fish, and other animals.
11. Use five sheets of computer paper, cut in half lengthwise, to make labels. Write with marker: 6 legs, body in 3 parts, usually 2 pairs of wings, usually 2 antennae, food for animals.

RECYCLING: HOW CAN I HELP?

MATERIALS AND SUPPLIES

- orange cloth background
- yellow border
- yellow letters
- black paper
- pictures of things recyclable:
  steel and aluminum cans, plastic,
  paper, glass containers, tires,
  used motor oil, and old cars

- any white paper that crayons can write on
  (Used computer paper, clean on one side, is OK.)
- clear plastic bags
- aluminum soda cans
- newspaper
- pins or staples
- crayons
- scissors

INSTRUCTIONS

1. From face patterns on pages 64 to 67, choose two girls' faces and two boys' faces. Color heavily and cut them out.
2. Using the hand pattern on page 67, color and cut out five hands.
3. Make a tire by tracing around a dinner plate on black paper. Cut out the center.
4. Fold a page or two of newspaper so it fits beneath the boy's hand. Use straight pins or staples to hold the newspaper in place.
5. Use four or five plastic bags to pin or staple beneath the first girl's hand.
6. Place several used aluminum soda cans in a plastic bag and pin or staple it in place under the hand.
7. Pin or staple the tire above two hands.
8. Discuss recycling: the process of making new things from used things instead of throwing them into landfill holes in the ground.
9. We can help by recycling trash, such as cans, glass, and paper, as much as possible.
10. We must never throw trash on the ground.
11. Ask the children to watch for trash that is thrown on the ground. Do not ask them to pick things up. They are simply to make lists of what they see and share the lists with the class.
12. Let the children help you find pictures of recyclable items and put them on the bulletin board.
13. After the children bring in their lists of items thrown on the ground, let them draw pictures of these things. Put the pictures on the bulletin board.

MATERIALS AND SUPPLIES

- dark-blue cloth background
- white border
- white letters
- crayons
- glue
- any white paper that crayons can write on
  (Used computer paper, clean on one side is OK.)
- scissors
- wide-tipped black marker

INSTRUCTIONS

1. From the patterns on pages 89 and 95, color the woman's head, arm, and hand. Cut and tape them together (so the head can be used again).
2. Make a boy's head and neck only, reversed, from the pattern on page 101. Add an arm from page 67. Color and tape them together.
3. Make a white "balloon." Write the words with the wide marker.
4. Discuss the importance of saying "thank you" at home and at school, or anywhere someone does something for you.
5. Let the children tell when saying "thank you" is appropriate: when someone does something for us or gives us something. Some of those who help us are the school lunch workers who serve us our food, our teacher who gives us something, the librarian who hands us our library books, the bus driver who stops to let us off at our home or a bus stop, and cashiers who serve us at stores. Many times each day we can say "thank you" to those who do something for us or help us, and we can add a smile too. Mothers and fathers do more things for us than anyone and they like to hear those two words also.
6. Let the children make simple thank-you letters for their mothers and fathers. Tell them thank you for their care. List things such as cooking food, washing clothes, cleaning the house, mowing the lawn, washing the car, fixing things, working so we can have a home.
7. If children can't write, let them draw "thank-you" pictures showing things their parents do for them.
8. The children can draw pictures of things for which they need to tell others "thank you." Put these on the bulletin board or around it.

MATERIALS AND SUPPLIES

- dark-green cloth background
- white border, edged with orange marker
- white letters, edged with orange marker
- crayons
- scissors
- any white paper that crayons can write on (Used computer paper, clean on one side, is OK.)
- wide-tipped orange marker
- transparent tape

INSTRUCTIONS

1. Using the pattern on page 99, make the boy, hand, and question mark. Color as desired. Tape the hand lightly in place.
2. Ask the children to tell about a favorite place where they like to go: a comfortable room or chair, the library, a friend's house, or their grandparents' house; or an outdoor place, such as a porch swing, pool, ballpark, tree house, or fishing spot.
3. Give the children each a piece of paper. Let them draw themselves in their favorite place, doing what they enjoy most. Outline each scene with orange marker.
4. If the children can write, let them write about their favorite place and draw a picture of it.
5. Display the children's pictures and writing on the bulletin board and tape extras on the wall.

MATERIALS AND SUPPLIES

- dark-blue cloth background
- yellow border
- yellow letters
- jar or can labels
- cash register receipts (optional)
- pictures of grocery items from store ads or newspaper ads
- any white paper that crayons can write on (Used computer paper, clean on one side, is OK.)
- wide-tipped black marker
- crayons
- scissors
- glue

INSTRUCTIONS

1. From the pattern on page 96, color and cut out the boy and shoes. Glue the shoes to the boy's legs on the dotted lines. (Omit the boy's right arm.)
2. Use the pattern on page 87 for the cart. Color and cut it out.
3. Ask the children what supermarkets have. List their responses on the chalkboard.
4. Let the children draw pictures of people working in a supermarket.
5. Ask the children to bring in jar or can labels from things that were bought at a supermarket, as well as cash register receipts (optional), pictures from grocery ads, or newspaper ads.
6. Put pictures, labels, and so on, on and around the bulletin board.
7. Let the children role-play jobs that workers perform in a supermarket. As each performs, let the rest of the class guess what job he or she is acting out.

MATERIALS AND SUPPLIES

- dark-blue cloth background (Used computer paper, clean on one side, is OK.)
- transparent tape
- crayons
- scissors
- white letters
- white border
- white computer paper
- wide-tipped black marker

INSTRUCTIONS

1. Ask the children to think of safety rules we all should follow. Write them on the chalkboard:
   Wear seat belts. Look both ways before crossing the street. Keep both hands on the handlebars of a bicycle. Remove toys from steps. Keep away from moving swings. Keep wet hands away from electric light switches. Don't tease dogs, and don't pet dogs you don't know. Keep hands inside moving cars. Learn to swim. Bicycle with care. Don't talk to strangers. Don't play with matches. Be aware of things that can be poisonous in your home, and don't touch or taste them.
2. Print some safety rules on white computer paper and put them on the bulletin board.
3. Color and cut out safety items from these patterns:
   girl and road, p. 90; water drops, p. 91; boy and electric switch, p. 91; dog and boy in water, p. 91; car and steps, p. 106; seat belt, p. 110
4. Let the children draw safety pictures. Outline them with marker and tape them to the wall.

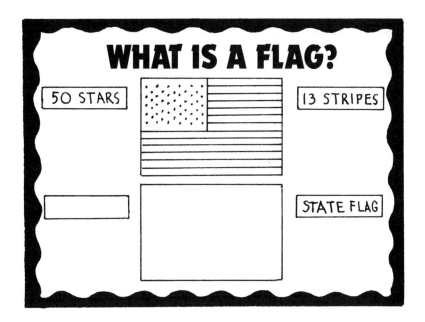

MATERIALS AND SUPPLIES

- light-blue cloth background
- dark-blue border
- dark-blue letters
- an American flag
- a state flag (optional)
- 2 sheets of computer paper
- any white paper that crayons can write on (Used computer paper, clean on one side, is OK.)
- crayons
- scissors
- wide-tipped black marker

INSTRUCTIONS

1. Display the United States flag. (As an option, let the children each make a flag. Choose one or two and put them on the bulletin board.)
2. Place the flag of your state under the American flag, or let the children each make one and choose one for the bulletin board.
3. Make four labels from two sheets of computer paper cut in half lengthwise. Print with the marker: 50 stars, 13 stripes, (name of your state), state flag
4. Ask the children why our country's flag is important: The flag is a symbol of our country and of freedom. We honor it because we are free to choose jobs, homes, religion, and leaders for our country.
5. Out of respect for our flag, we must never let it touch the ground. It must be folded carefully when it is taken from the flagpole.
6. Ask the children what their state flag looks like. Tell them it is a symbol of their state and the people who have worked hard to make it a good state.
7. Factories, schools, government buildings (such as the courthouse and post office) display flags in front of, or on top of, the buildings every day.
8. When a very important person of our country dies, flags are flown only halfway up the flagpole ("half mast") in honor of that person.
9. Get a children's book about our first flag, such as *The American Flag* by Ann Armbruster or *Our Flag* by Eleanor Ayer, and read it to the children.
10. With the children, count the stars on our flag. Each one stands for a state in the United States. Count the thirteen red and white stripes. They stand for the first thirteen colonies in our country.
11. Take a walk to look at the flag in front of, or on top of, your school, if your school displays one.
12. Let the children make flags from other countries and share them with the class.

WHAT IS A FAIR?

MATERIALS AND SUPPLIES

- dark-brown cloth background
- white border
- white letters
- crayons

- any white paper that crayons can write on
  (Used computer paper, clean on one side, is OK.)
- scissors

INSTRUCTIONS

1. From the pattern on page 97, make a Ferris wheel. Color and cut it out around the outer edges.
2. Using the patterns, color and cut out:
   pig, cow, and chicken, p. 82; sheep, p. 83; lamp and bread, p. 63; cheese, p. 81; jacket, p. 62; carrot, p. 92; pumpkin, p. 106; potato, p. 109
3. Discuss fairs with the children. Ask the children if they have been to one. Ask what things they saw and what they liked best. Write these things on the chalkboard: rides, exhibits (ribbons awarded), games, animals (ribbons awarded), races, food, vegetable and fruit displays, clothing and cake displays, advertisements, farm equipment, tractor pulls, and so on.
4. Ask the children to write about the fair and draw pictures of the things they liked best.
5. Children whose families have exhibited animals can tell and write about their experiences.
6. Display the children's stories and art work around the bulletin board.

PROJECT PATTERNS

TOOTH-
BRUSH

BOY, TOWEL,
CARROTS,
TOOTHBRUSH,
HANDS

CARROTS

BOY

TOWEL

HANDS

GIRL, FLOWER, ROOT, NAIL, BUTTON MOUTH

NAIL

GIRL

BUTTON
MOUTH

ROOT

FLOWER

BOY, CAP, TELEVISION GLASSES BEARD

BOY

TELEVISION

BEARD

CAP

GLASSES

60

GIRL

TREE
TRUNK

SUN

CAKE

61

BOY, APPLE, JACKET, BOOTS, SIX

BOY

SIX

APPLE

BOOTS

JACKET

GIRL, BREAD, HAM, LAMP

GIRL

HAM

BREAD

LAMP

FACES, TELEPHONE, CORD, SAD EYEBROWS

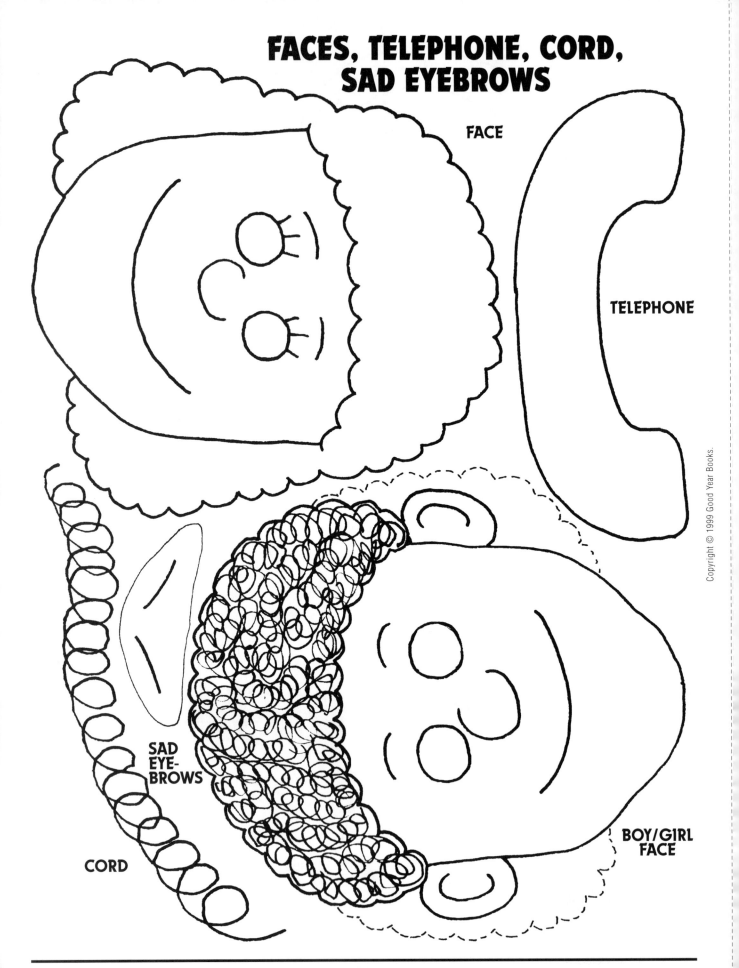

FACE

TELEPHONE

SAD
EYE-
BROWS

CORD

BOY/GIRL
FACE

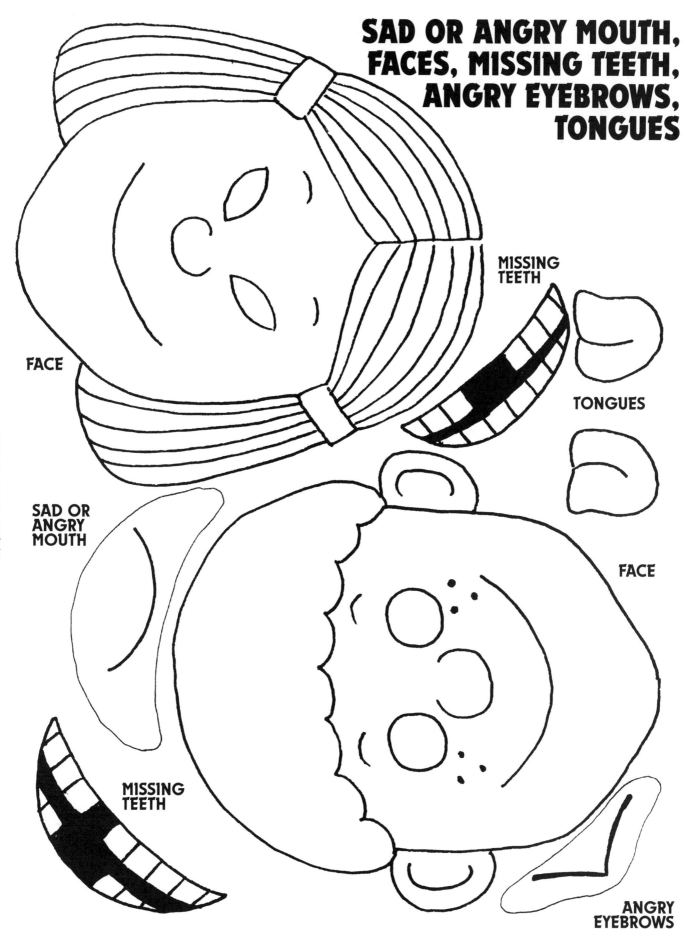

SAD OR ANGRY MOUTH,
FACES, MISSING TEETH,
ANGRY EYEBROWS,
TONGUES

MISSING TEETH

FACE

TONGUES

SAD OR ANGRY MOUTH

FACE

MISSING TEETH

ANGRY EYEBROWS

FACES, MOUTH, CIRCLE EYE, PAN, OVAL EYE

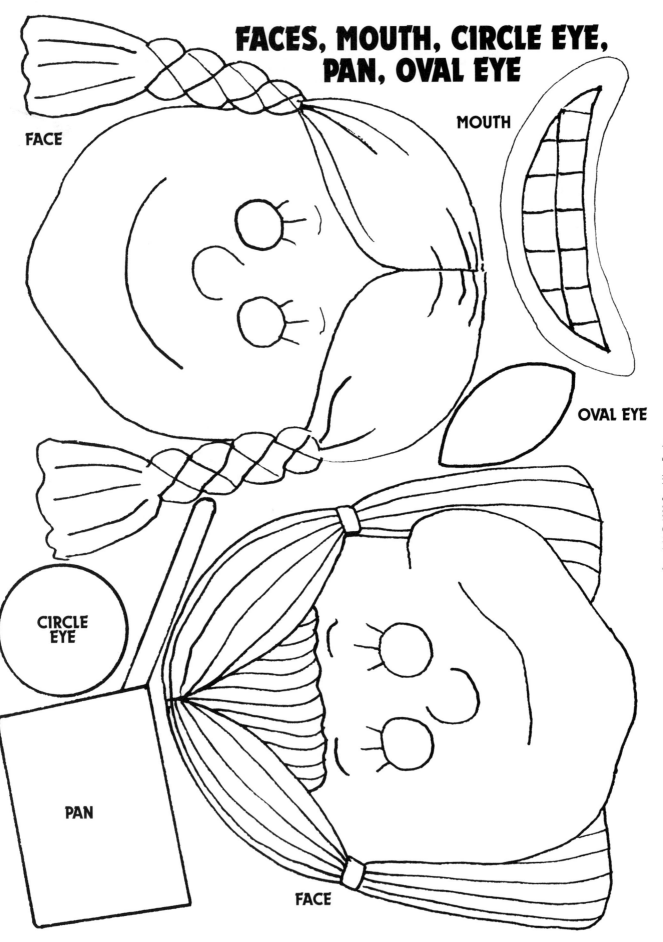

FACE

MOUTH

OVAL EYE

CIRCLE EYE

PAN

FACE

66

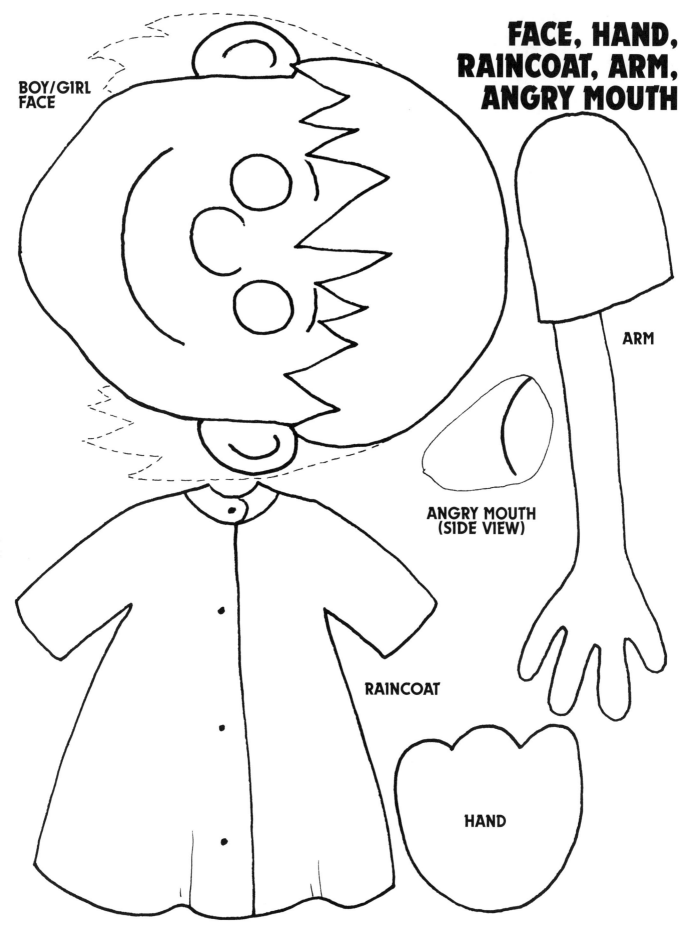

BOY/GIRL FACE

FACE, HAND,
RAINCOAT, ARM,
ANGRY MOUTH

ARM

ANGRY MOUTH
(SIDE VIEW)

RAINCOAT

HAND

HEART, BIRD, TREE, TREE TRUNK

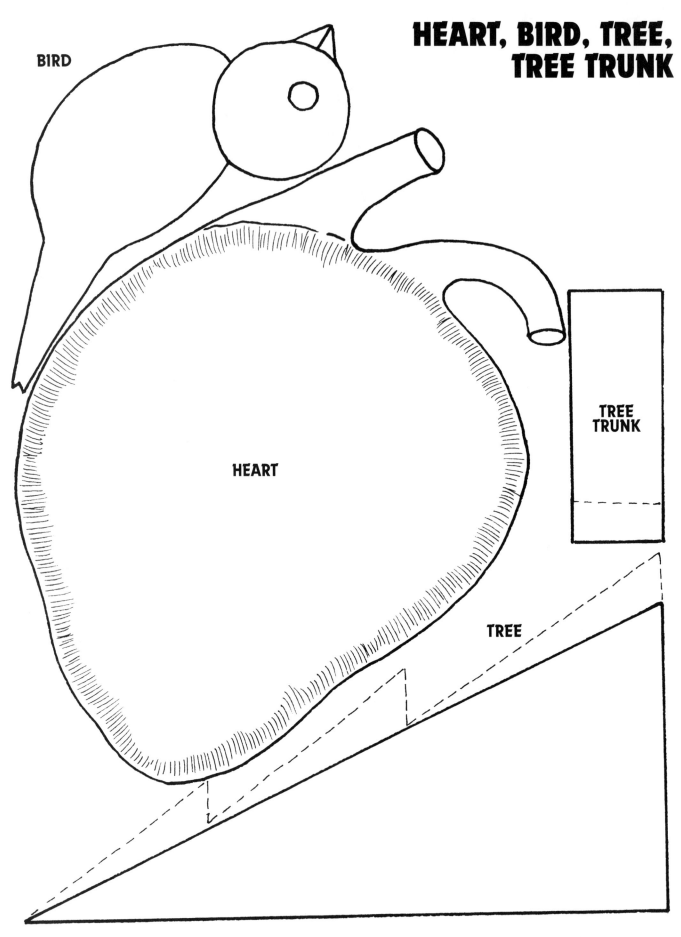

BIRD

HEART

TREE TRUNK

TREE

SNAKE, PUMPKIN

SNAKE

PUMPKIN

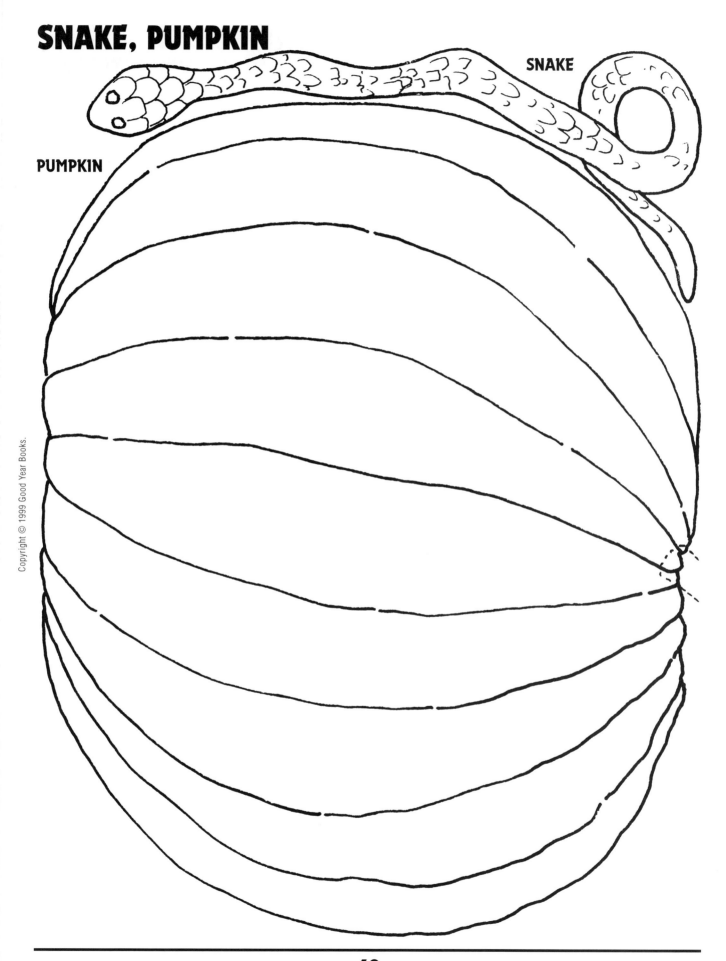

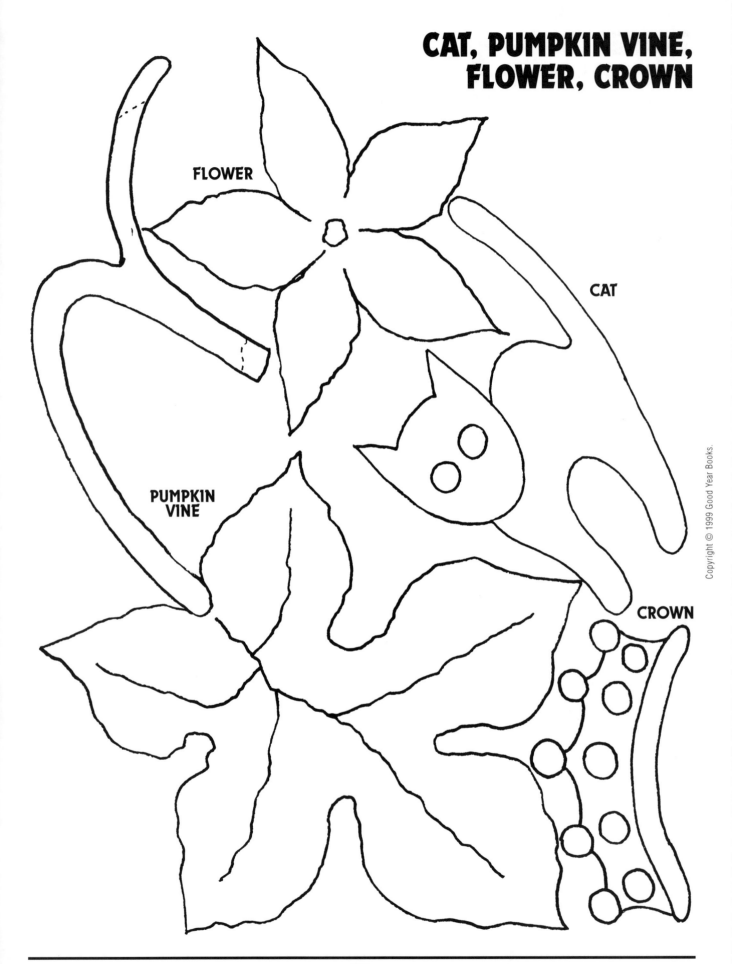

FLOWER

CAT

PUMPKIN VINE

CROWN

DESSERTS, HAND, SERIOUS MOUTH, ANGRY EYE

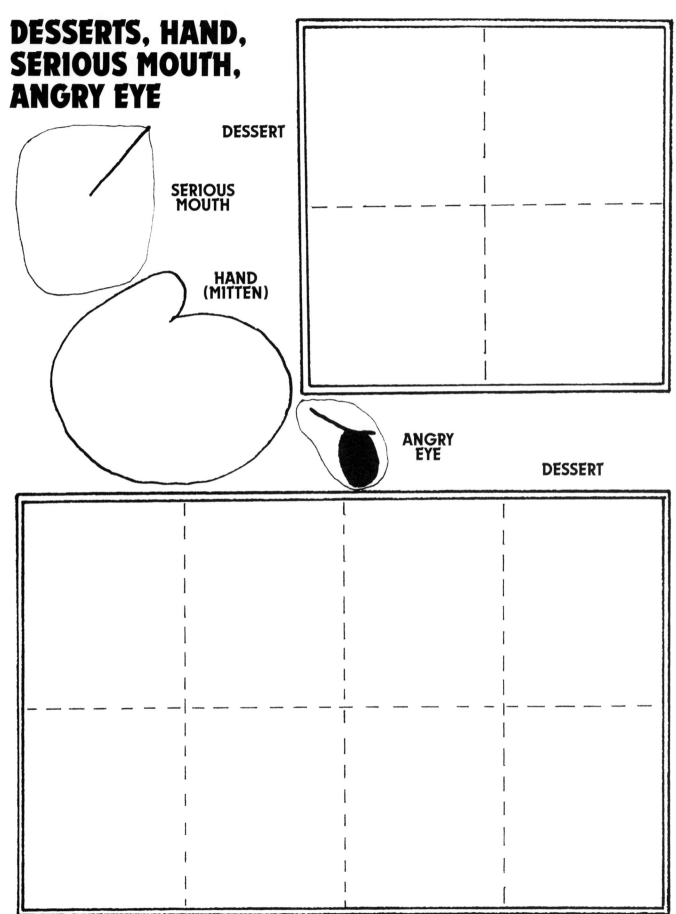

DESSERT

SERIOUS MOUTH

HAND (MITTEN)

ANGRY EYE

DESSERT

ORANGE-TREE TRUNK, ORANGE, SCARF, ORANGE TREE, EARMUFFS, PIE

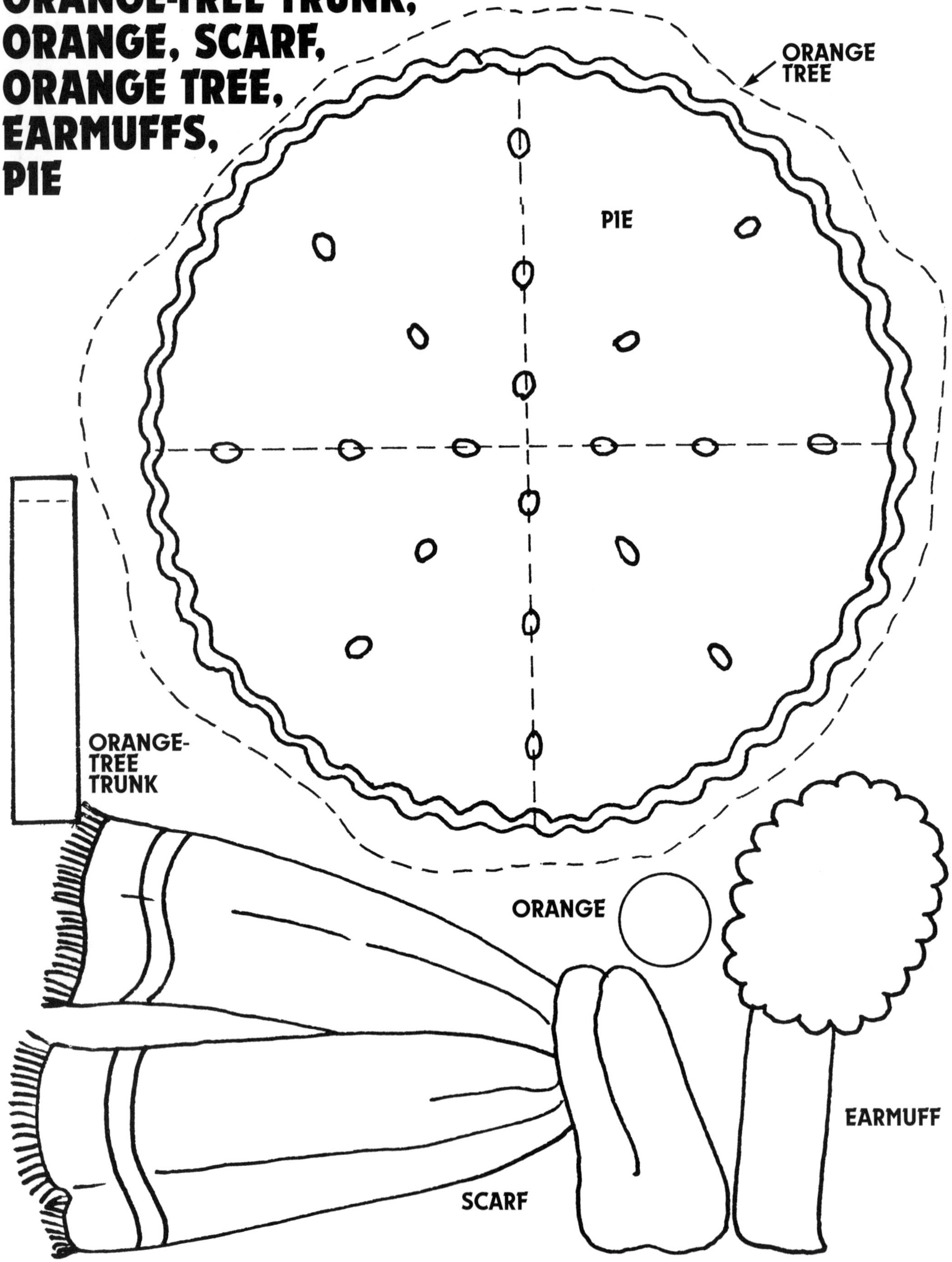

ORANGE TREE

PIE

ORANGE-TREE TRUNK

ORANGE

EARMUFF

SCARF

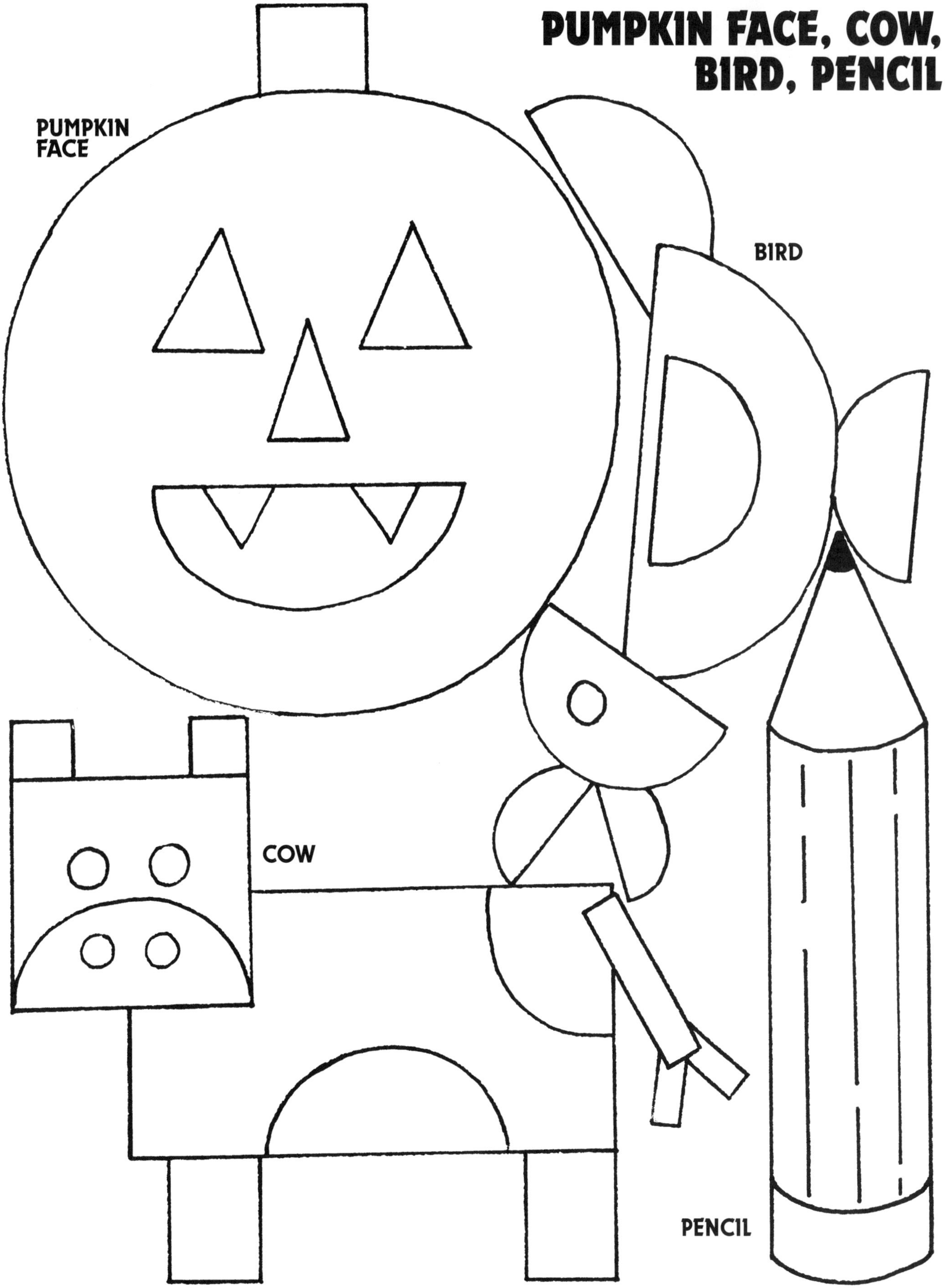

PUMPKIN
FACE

BIRD

COW

PENCIL

73

ROBOT, CUP, CAR,
GUMDROPS, CHIPMUNK,
SPIDER MONKEY,
MONKEY'S TAIL

ROBOT

MONKEY'S TAIL

CHIPMUNK

CUP

GUMDROPS

CAR

SPIDER MONKEY

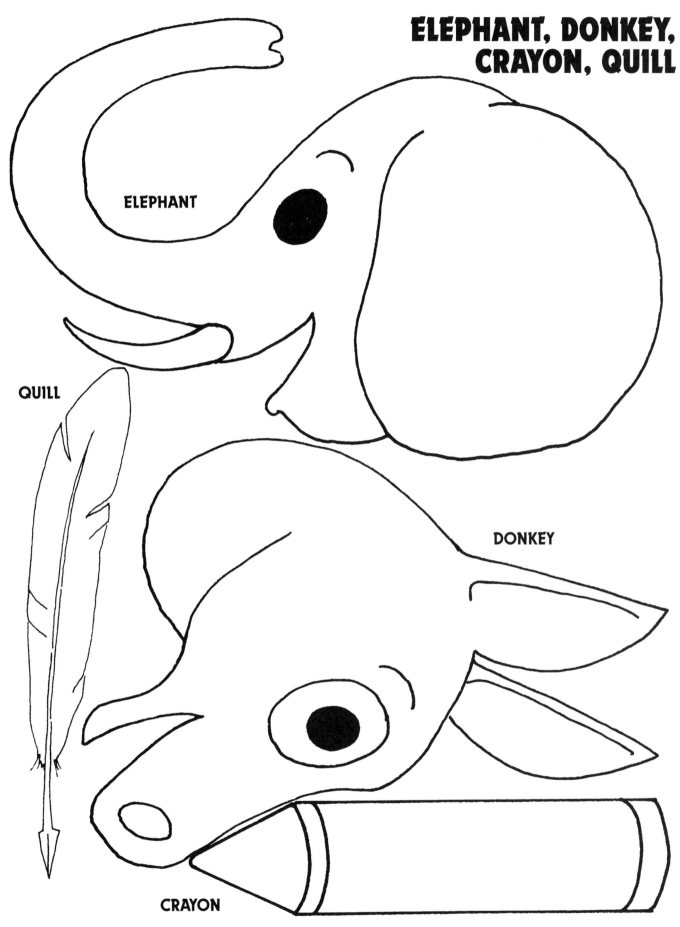

ELEPHANT

QUILL

DONKEY

CRAYON

DANNY DIBBY, LEG, ARM, EAR

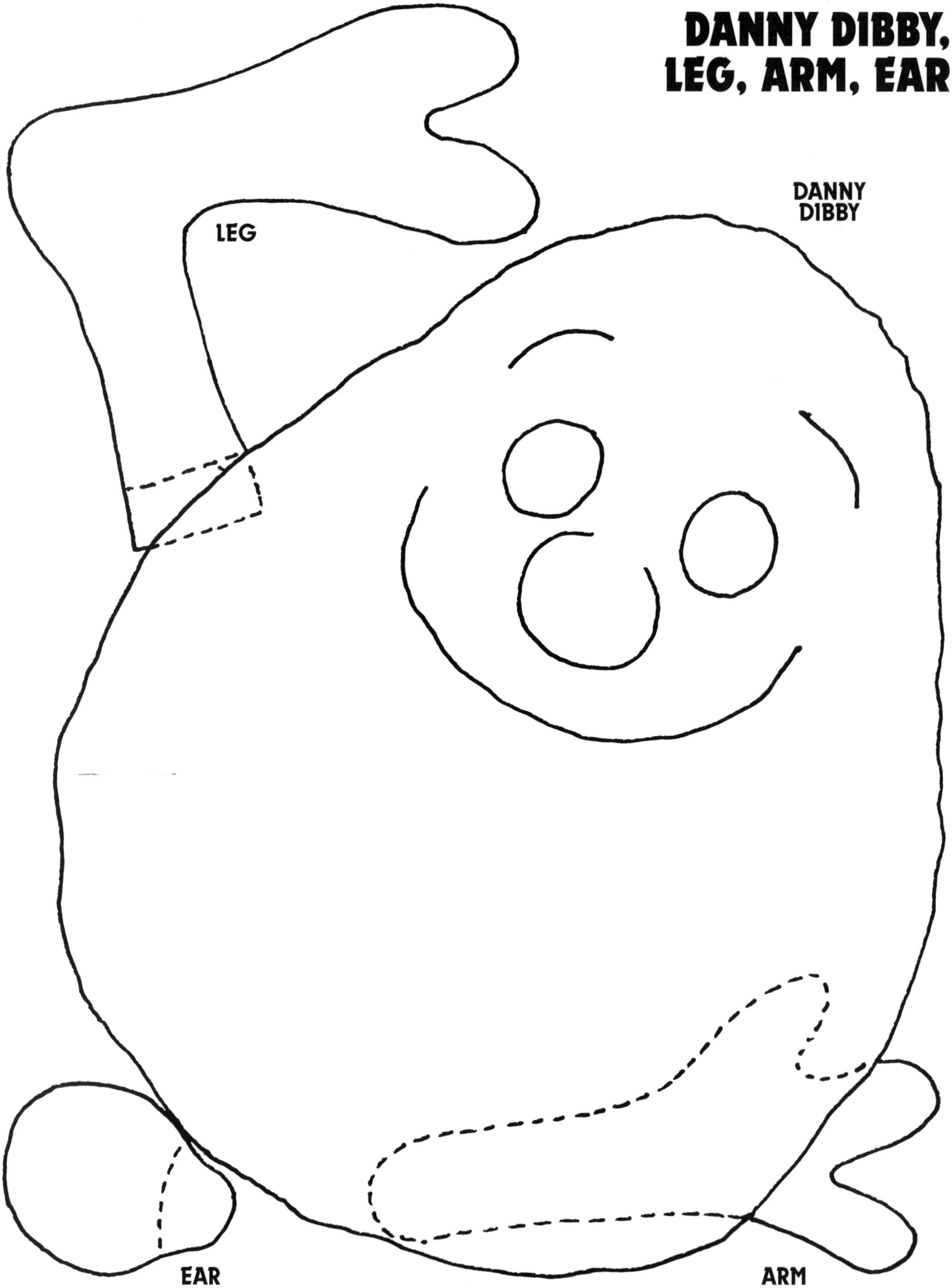

LEG

DANNY DIBBY

EAR

ARM

76

CAP

DANNY DIBBY

11

CATS, MARBLES, PALM-TREE TRUNK

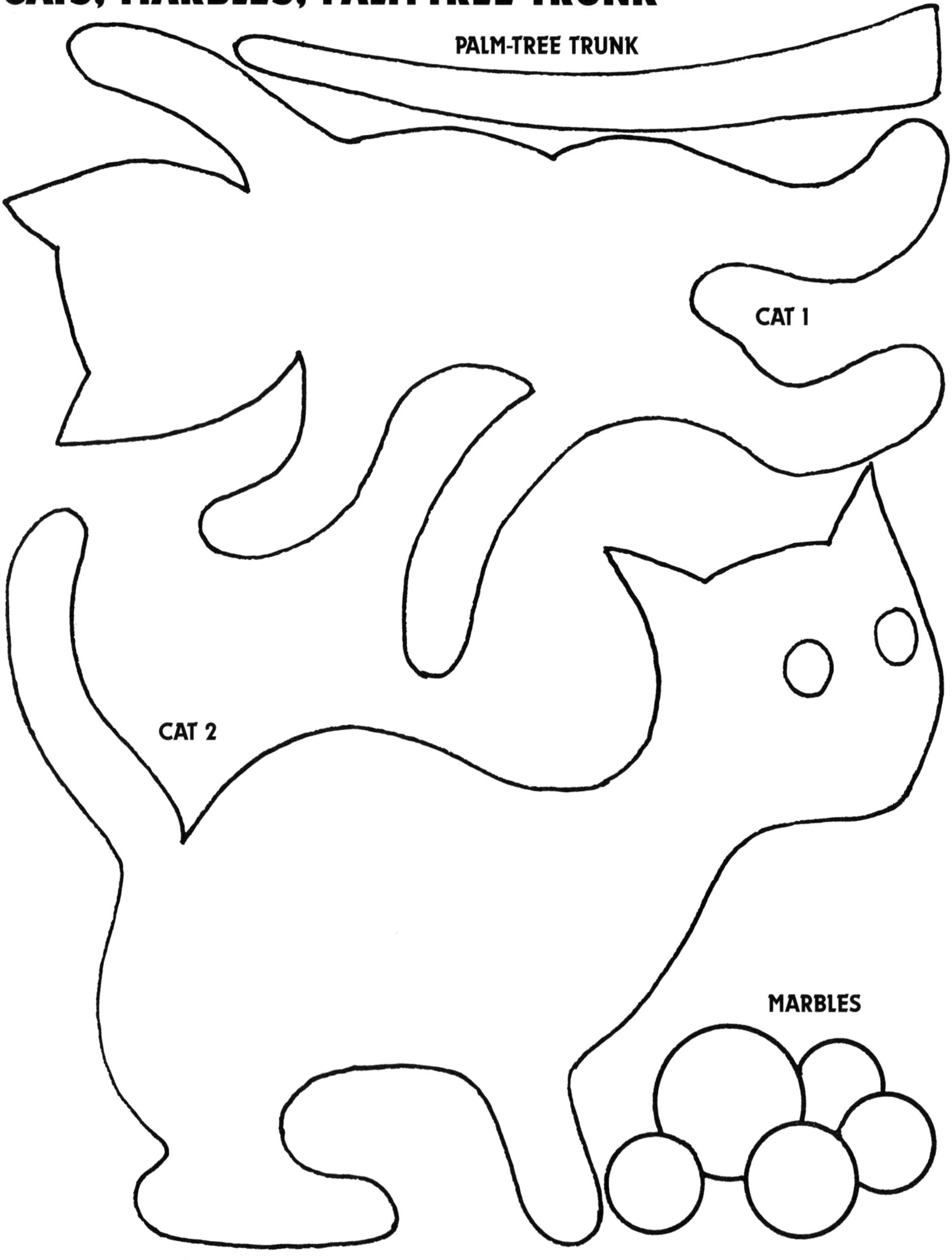

PALM-TREE TRUNK

CAT 1

CAT 2

MARBLES

CATS, VOLLEYBALL

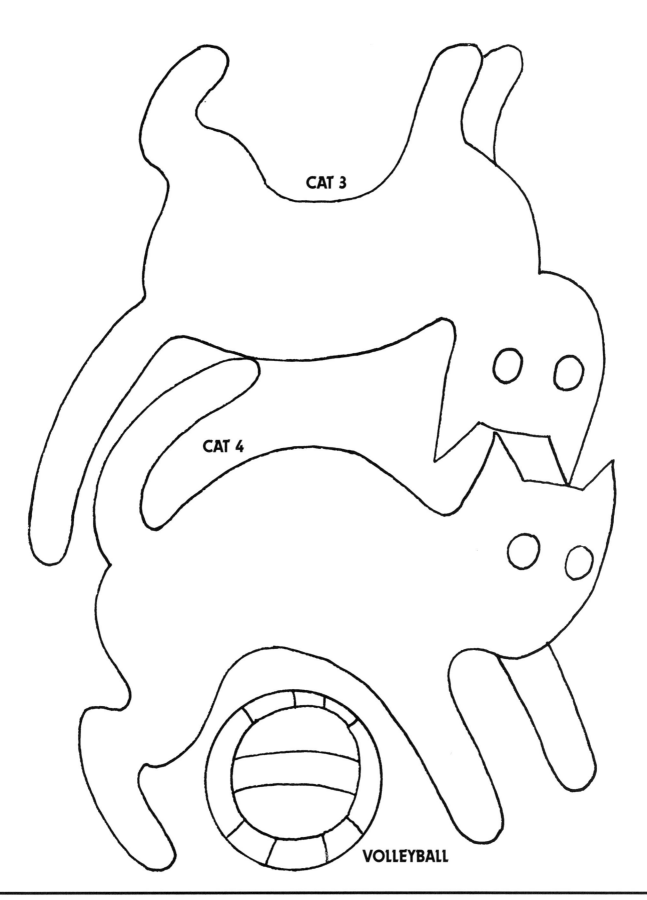

DAIRY, TRUCK, GRASS

GRASS

TRUCK

MILK
TANK TRUCK

DAIRY

DAIRY

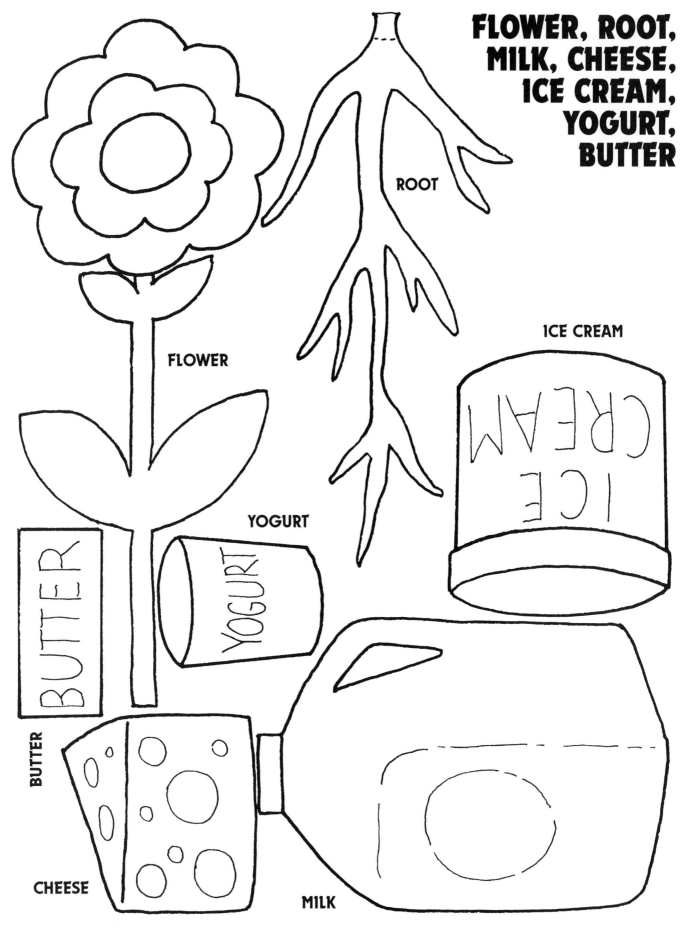

FLOWER, ROOT, MILK, CHEESE, ICE CREAM, YOGURT, BUTTER

ROOT

ICE CREAM

FLOWER

YOGURT

BUTTER

CHEESE

MILK

COW, PIG, CAT, CHICKEN

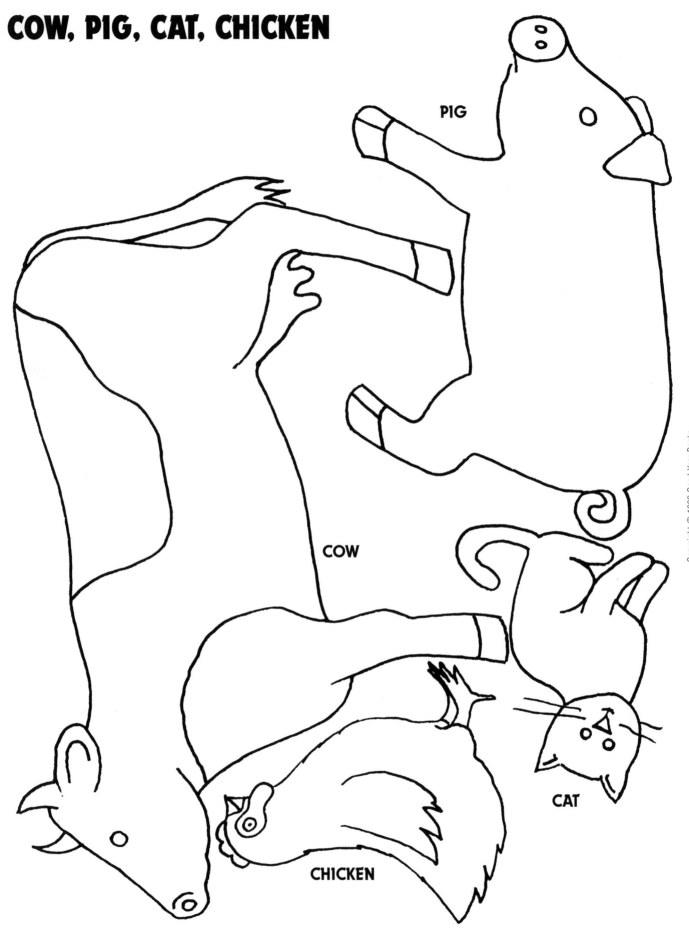

PIG

COW

CAT

CHICKEN

HORSE, SHEEP, PEPPER, KEY

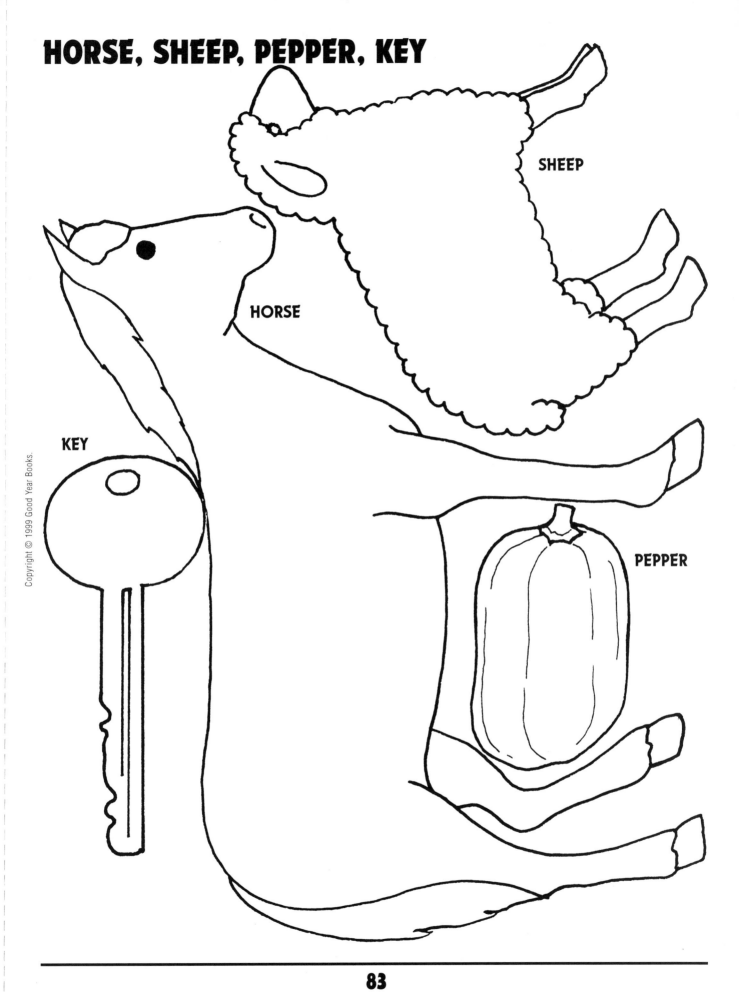

SHEEP

HORSE

KEY

PEPPER

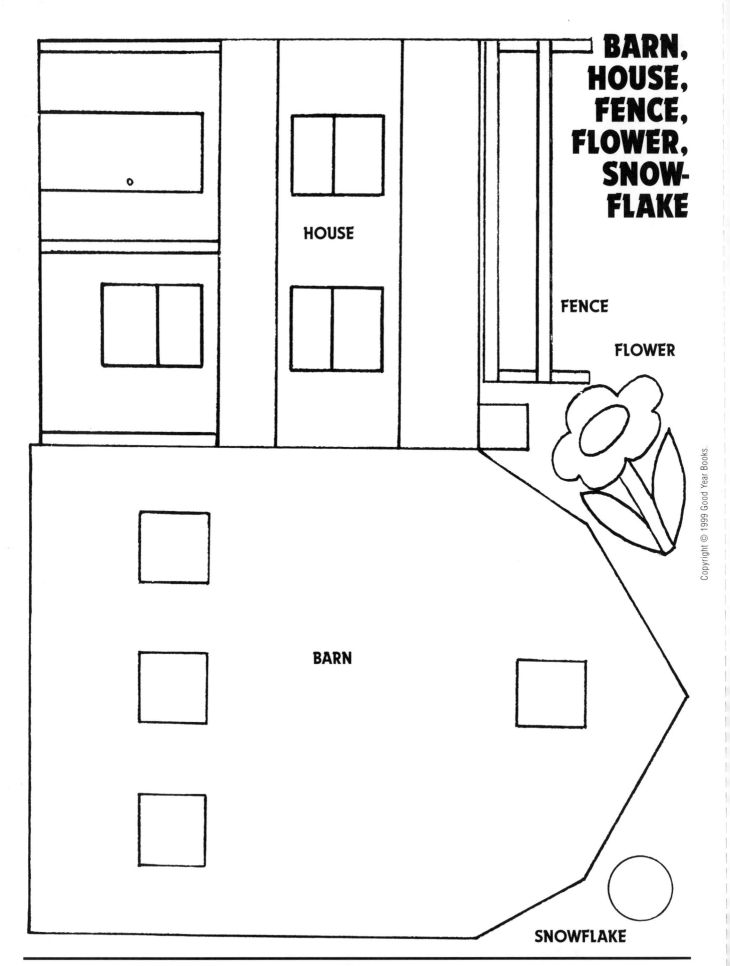

BARN,
HOUSE,
FENCE,
FLOWER,
SNOW-
FLAKE

HOUSE

FENCE

FLOWER

BARN

SNOWFLAKE

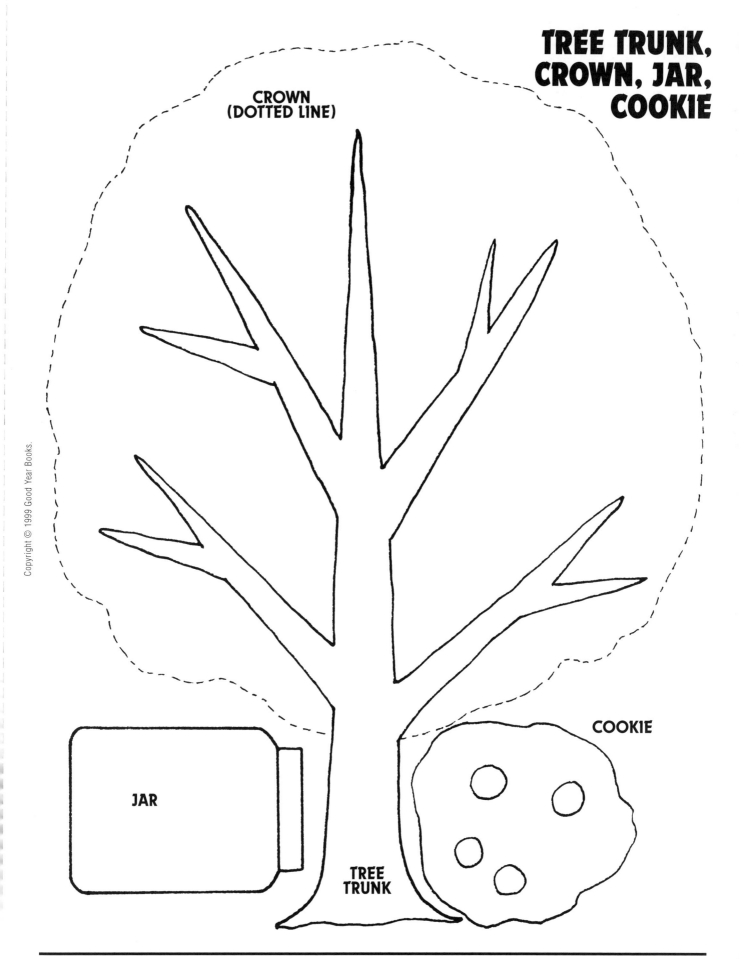

TREE TRUNK,
CROWN, JAR,
COOKIE

CROWN
(DOTTED LINE)

COOKIE

JAR

TREE
TRUNK

GUM

FOOT

TURKEY

TURKEY HEAD, LEGS, FEET, GROCERY CART, FEATHERS

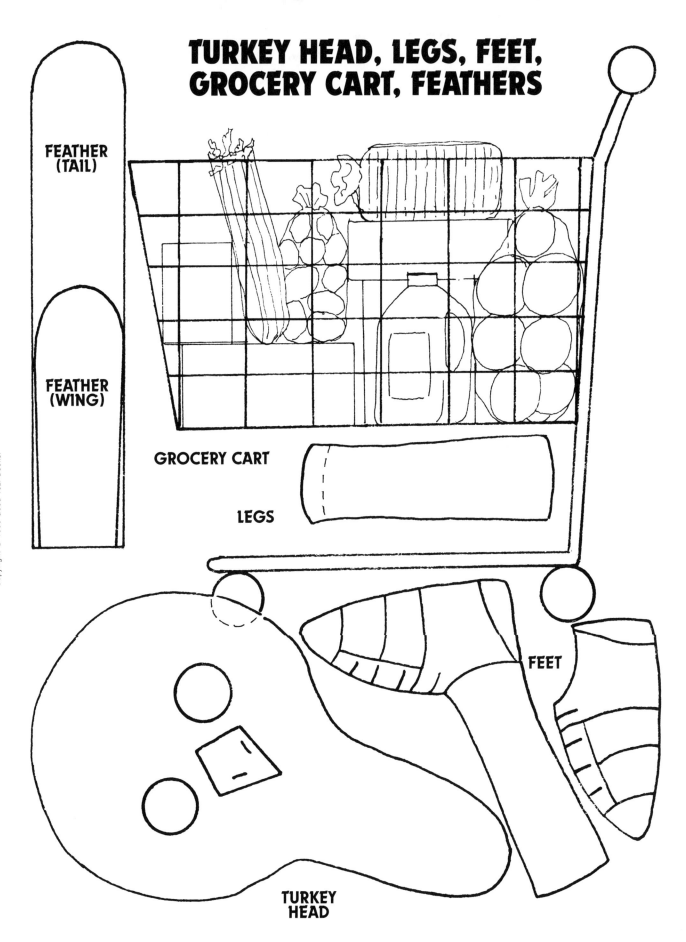

FEATHER
(TAIL)

FEATHER
(WING)

GROCERY CART

LEGS

FEET

TURKEY
HEAD

GEORGE WASHINGTON, SQUIRREL, ZIPPER

GEORGE
WASHINGTON

SQUIRREL
(FLYING
SQUIRREL—
DOTTED
LINE)

ZIPPER

UMBRELLA, HANDLE, ARM, HAND, WASHINGTON'S ARM

UMBRELLA
& HANDLE
(2 PARTS)

WOMAN'S
ARM

WOMAN'S
HAND

GEORGE
WASHINGTON'S
ARM

GIRL, ROAD, VOTING BOOTHS, DUCK

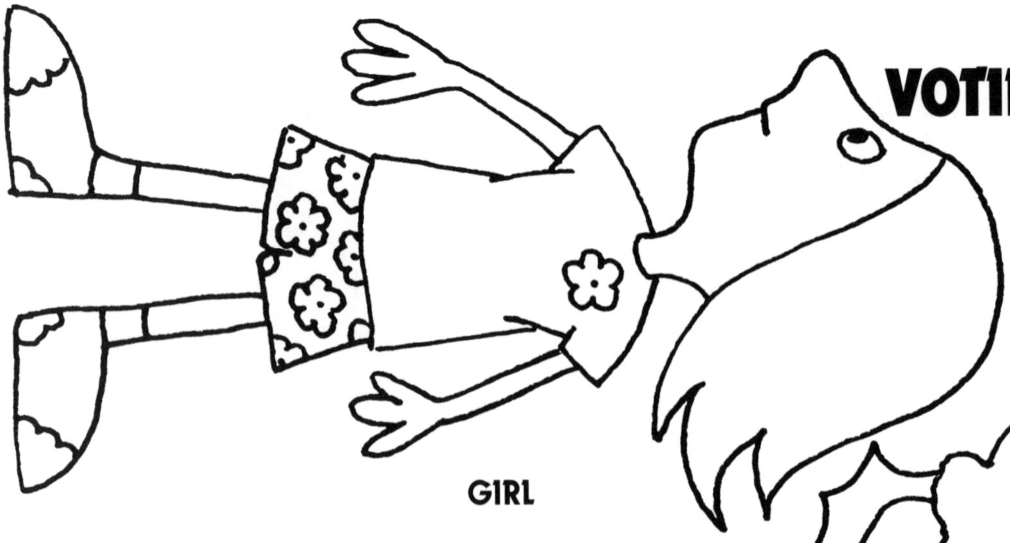

GIRL

DUCK

VOTING BOOTHS

ROAD

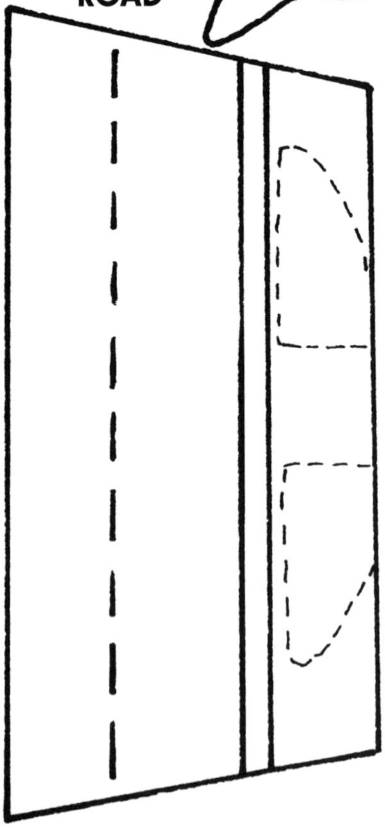

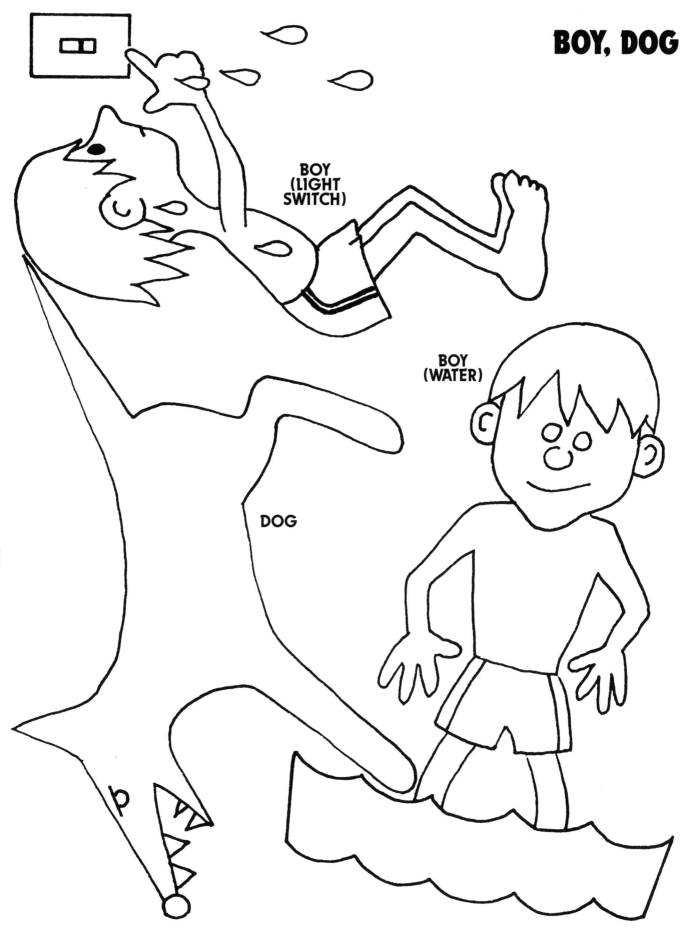

BOY
(LIGHT
SWITCH)

BOY
(WATER)

DOG

BIRD, CARROT, HAT, JUMPING ROPE

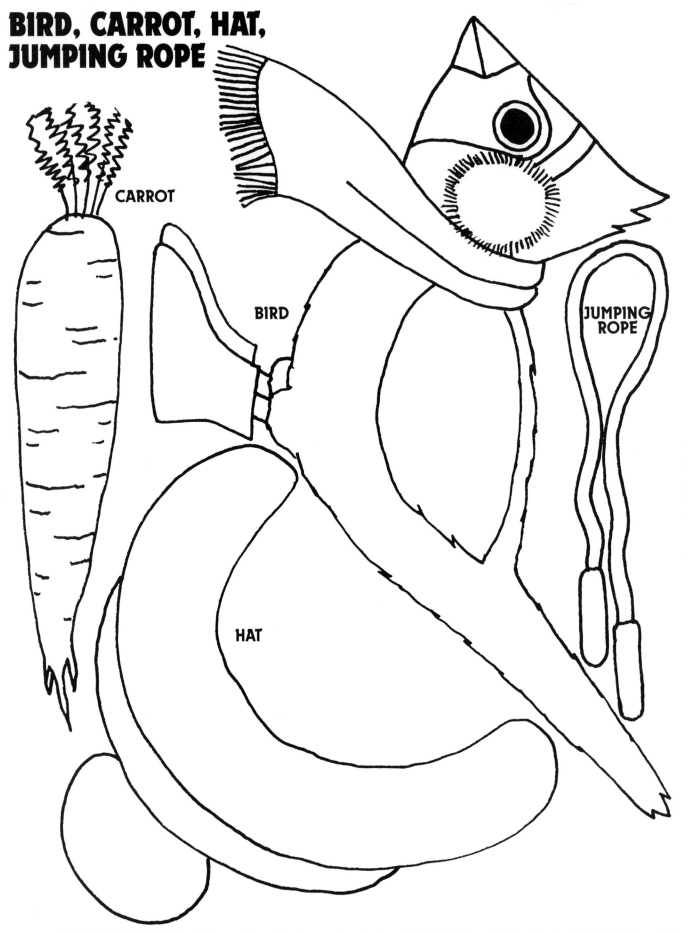

CARROT

BIRD

JUMPING ROPE

HAT

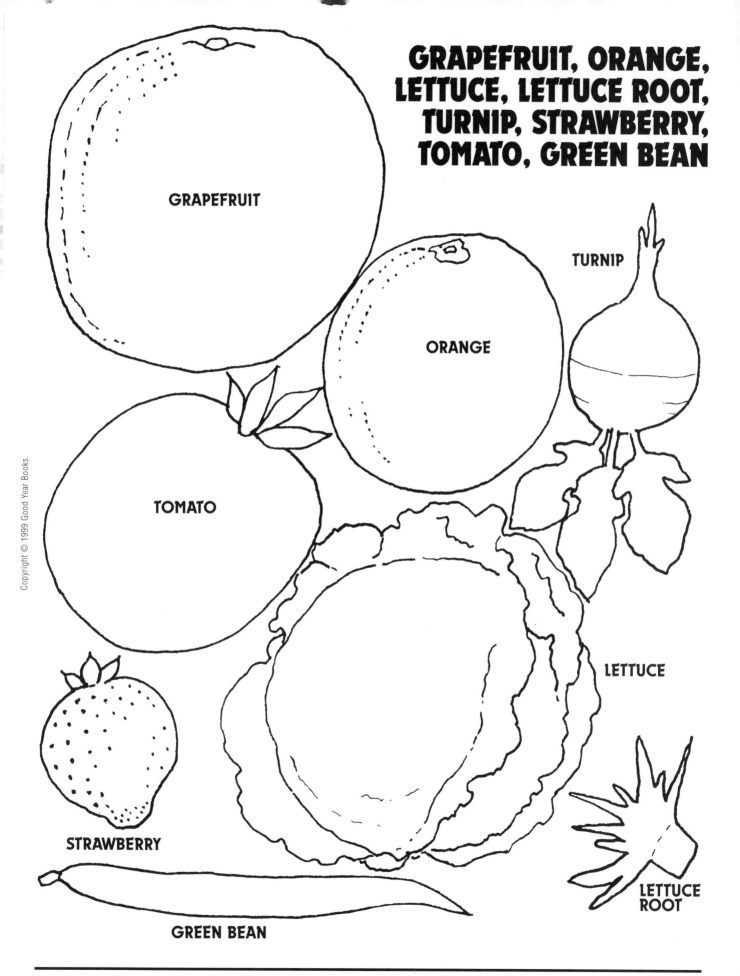

GRAPEFRUIT, ORANGE, LETTUCE, LETTUCE ROOT, TURNIP, STRAWBERRY, TOMATO, GREEN BEAN

GRAPEFRUIT

ORANGE

TURNIP

TOMATO

LETTUCE

STRAWBERRY

LETTUCE ROOT

GREEN BEAN

WEATHER SYMBOLS, POTATOES, HAT, RAIN HAT, SCARF

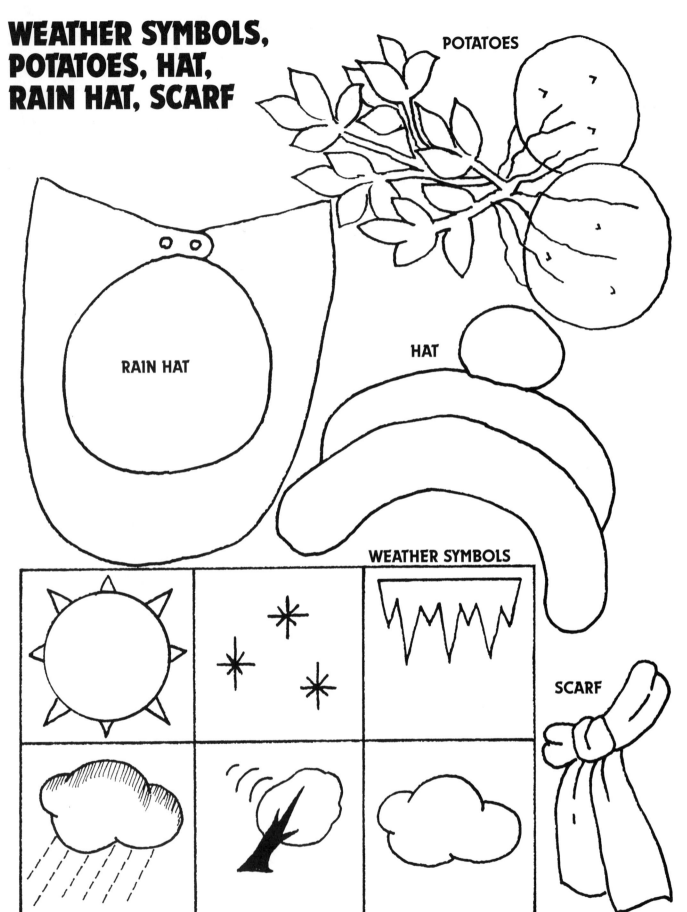

POTATOES

RAIN HAT

HAT

WEATHER SYMBOLS

SCARF

WOMAN, PEPPERS, CUPCAKE, ZERO, VINE

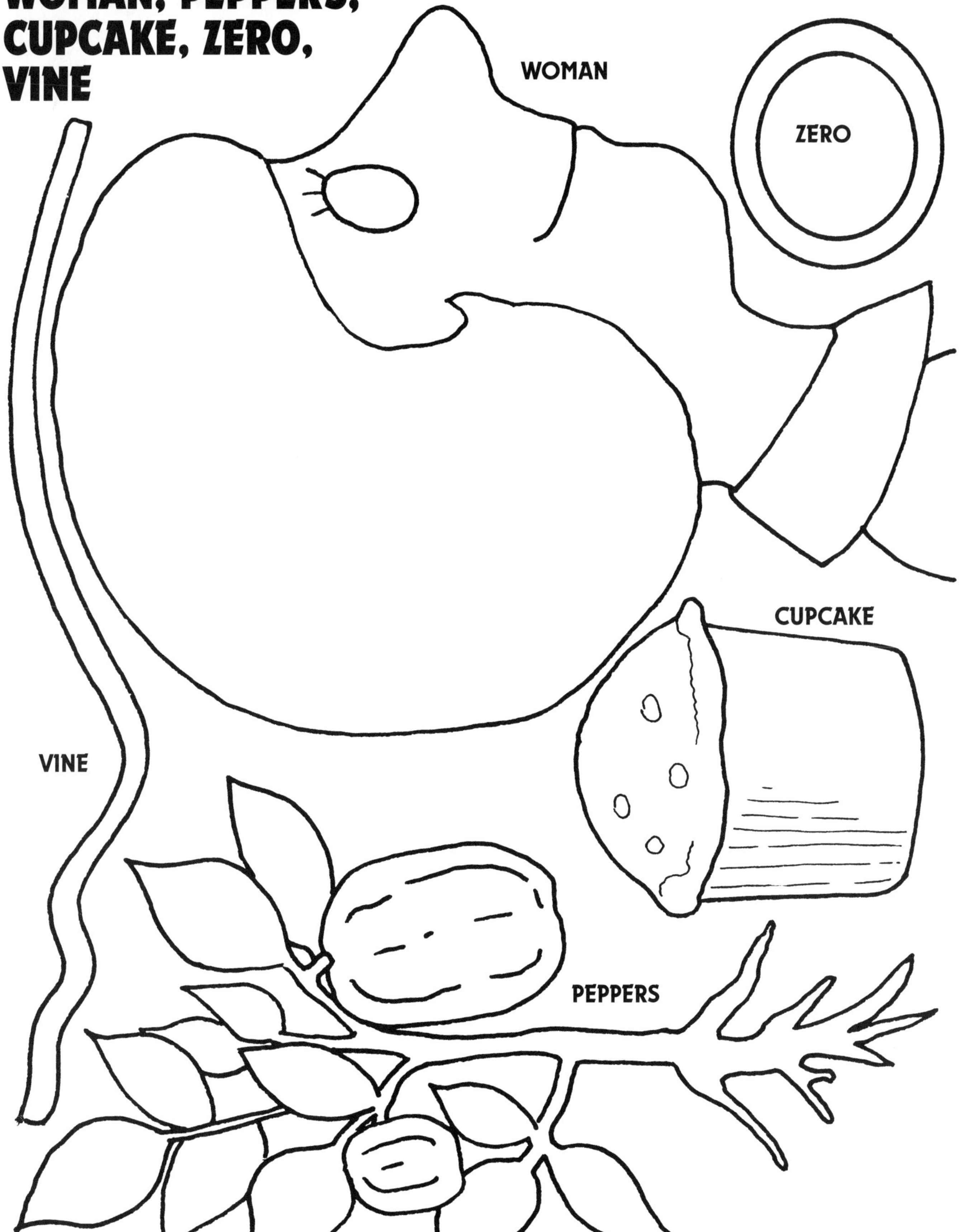

WOMAN

ZERO

CUPCAKE

VINE

PEPPERS

95

BOY, FEET, RADISH, BEET

RADISH

BOY

BEET

FEET

FERRIS WHEEL, TOMATO PLANT

TOMATO PLANT

FERRIS WHEEL

GREEN BEAN PLANT, INSECT, HEART

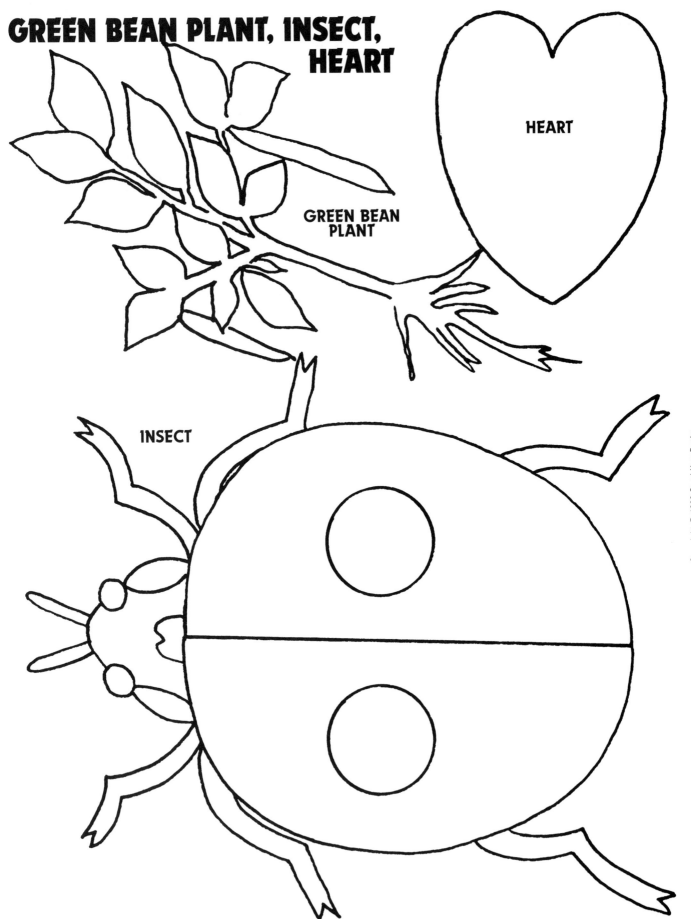

HEART

GREEN BEAN
PLANT

INSECT

FACE, HAND, QUESTION MARK, TOOTH, SEED, SPROUTS, BUD

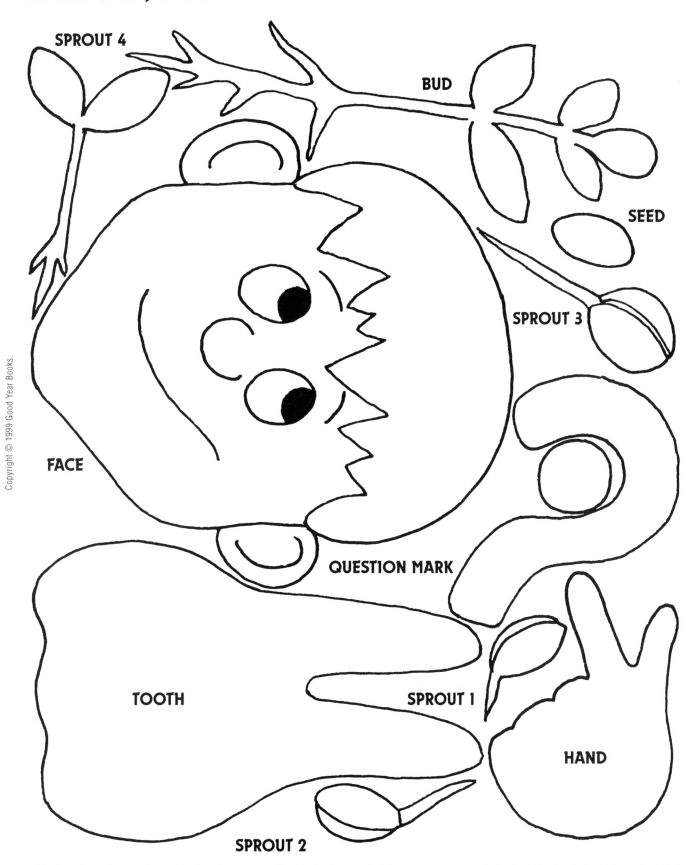

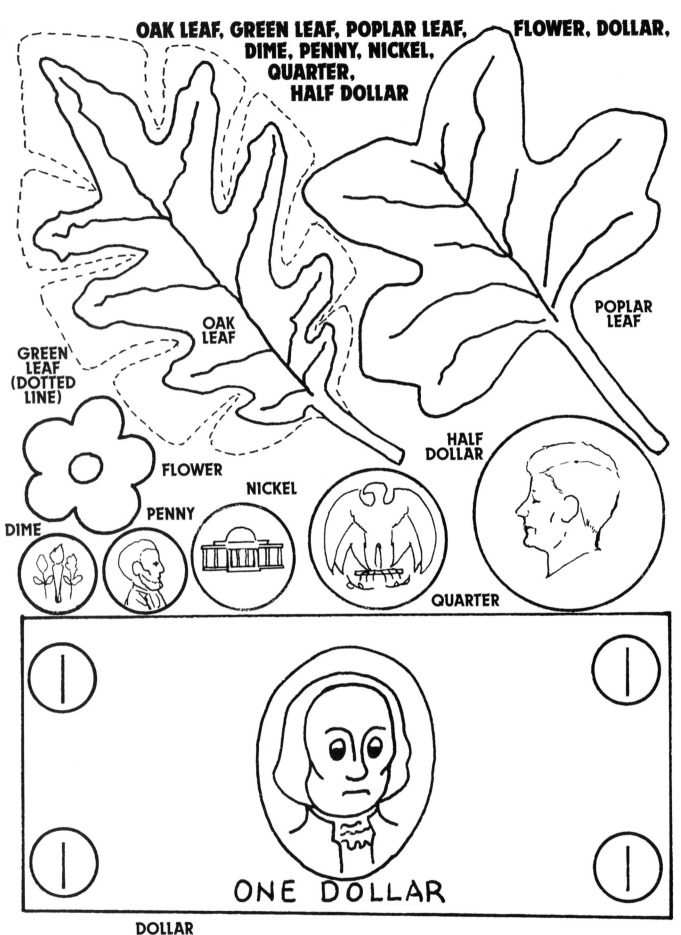

OAK LEAF, GREEN LEAF, POPLAR LEAF, FLOWER, DOLLAR, DIME, PENNY, NICKEL, QUARTER, HALF DOLLAR

POPLAR LEAF

OAK LEAF

GREEN LEAF (DOTTED LINE)

FLOWER

HALF DOLLAR

NICKEL

PENNY

DIME

QUARTER

ONE DOLLAR

DOLLAR

BOY/GIRL FACE, ARM, EYES

BOY FACE
(GIRL FACE-
DOTTED LINE)

ARM

EYES

BOY/GIRL BOTTOM, ARM, RAIN-FOREST LEAF, BANANA LEAF

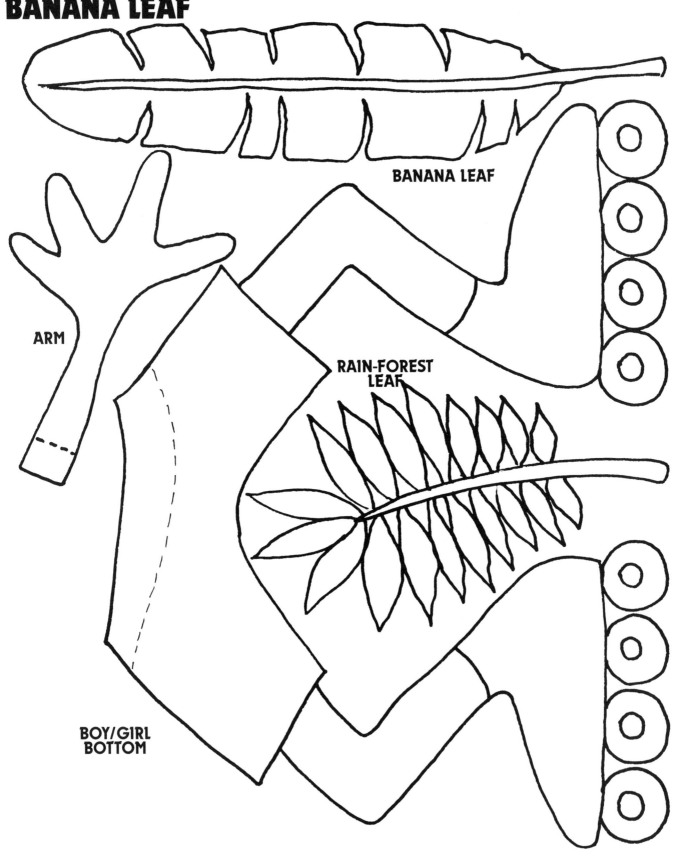

BANANA LEAF

ARM

RAIN-FOREST
LEAF

BOY/GIRL
BOTTOM

WATERMELON, PEAR, LEMON, PLUM, BANANA, KIWI, MANGO, RASPBERRY

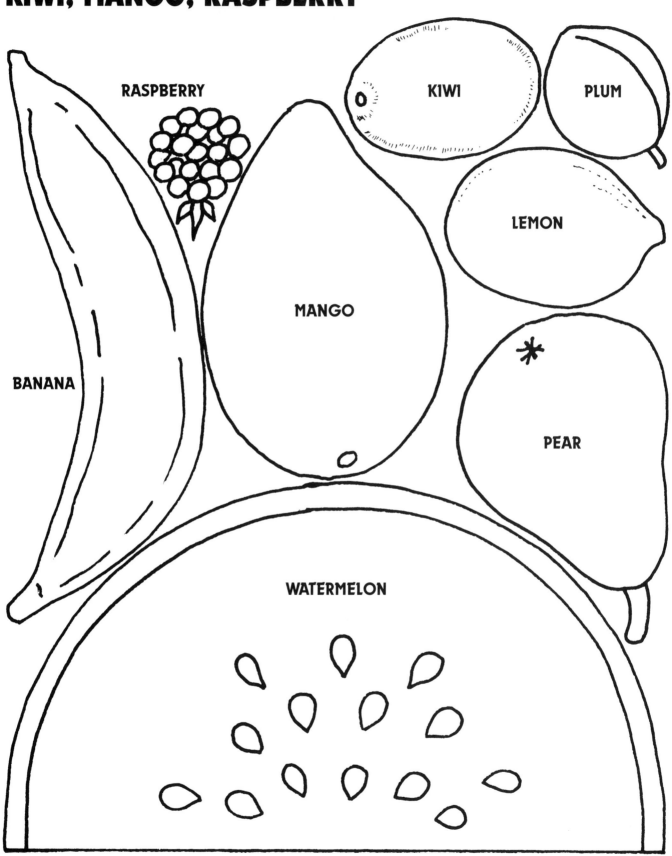

RASPBERRY

KIWI

PLUM

LEMON

MANGO

BANANA

PEAR

WATERMELON

SHIP

SHIP (BOTTOM)

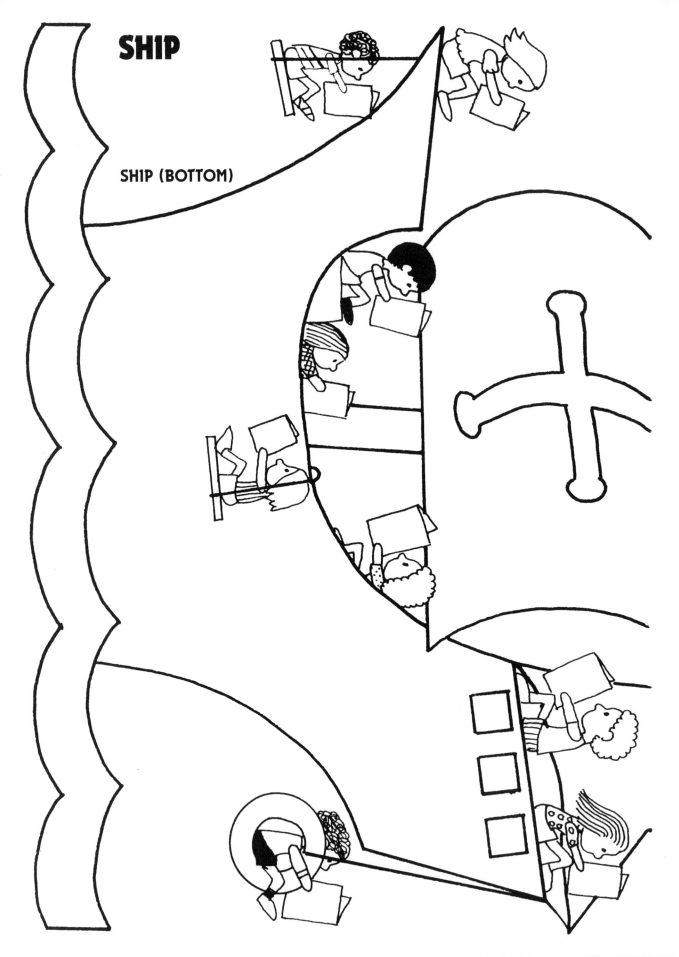

SHIP

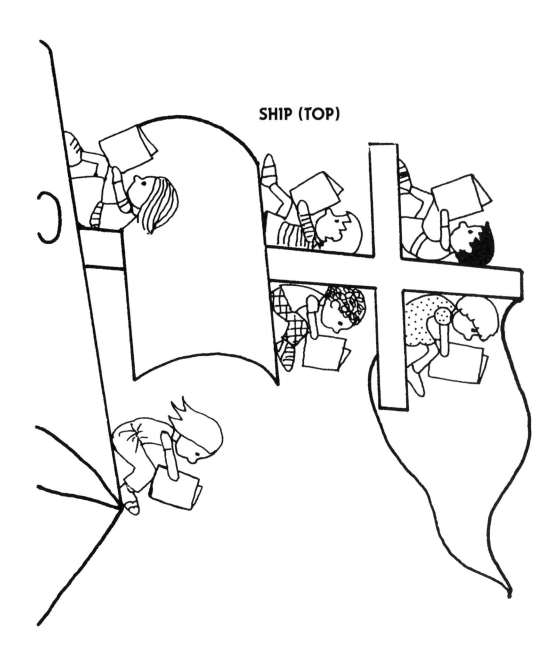

SHIP (TOP)

PUMPKIN, CAR, FISH, STEPS

PUMPKIN

STEPS

FISH

CAR

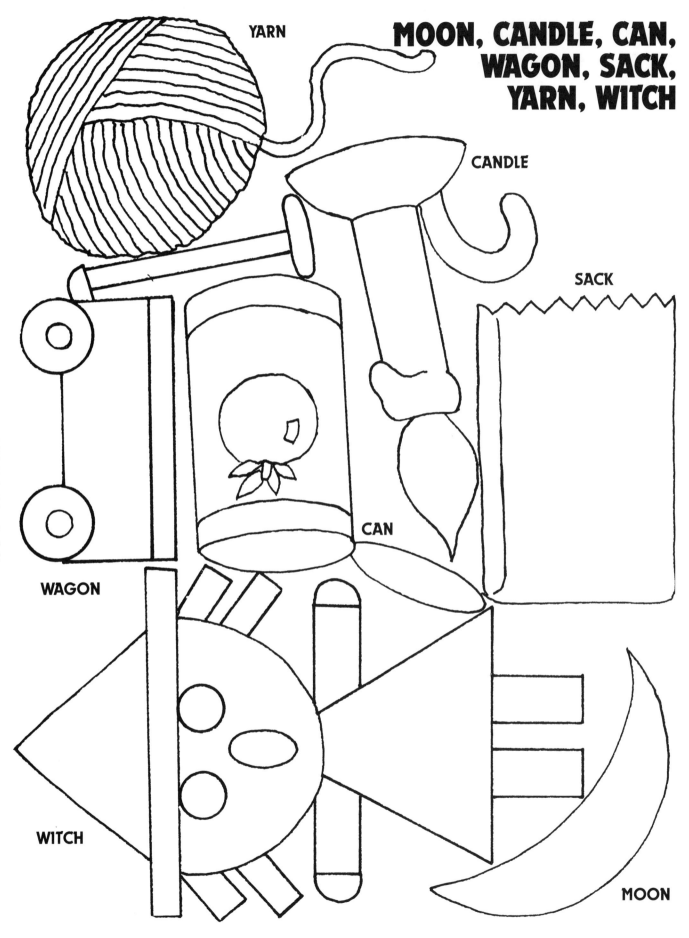

YARN

MOON, CANDLE, CAN,
WAGON, SACK,
YARN, WITCH

CANDLE

SACK

CAN

WAGON

WITCH

MOON

107

PALM LEAVES, BUTTERFLY, FROG, TOUCAN, CHRISTMAS CACTUS, SNAKE PLANT

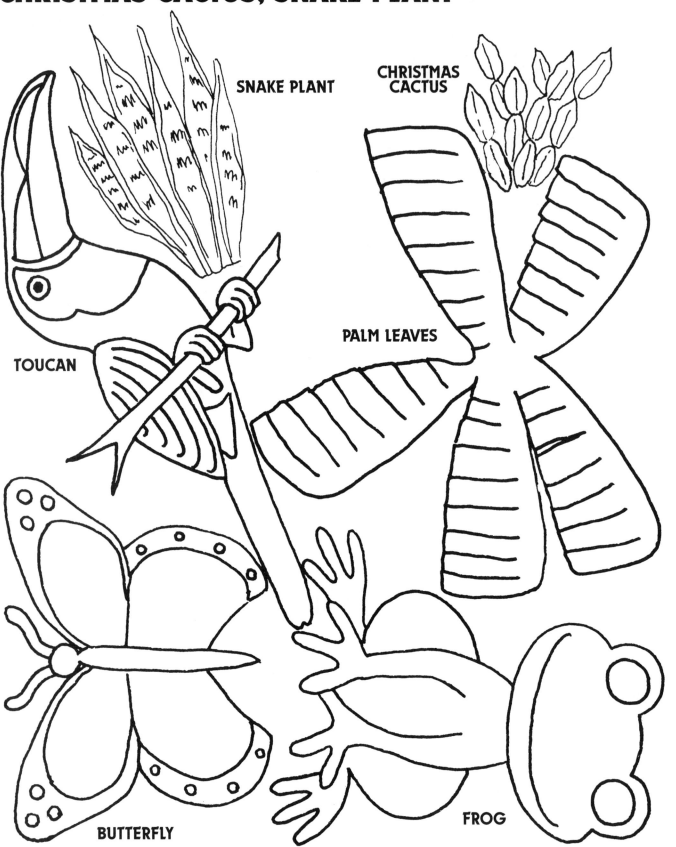

SNAKE PLANT

CHRISTMAS CACTUS

PALM LEAVES

TOUCAN

BUTTERFLY

FROG

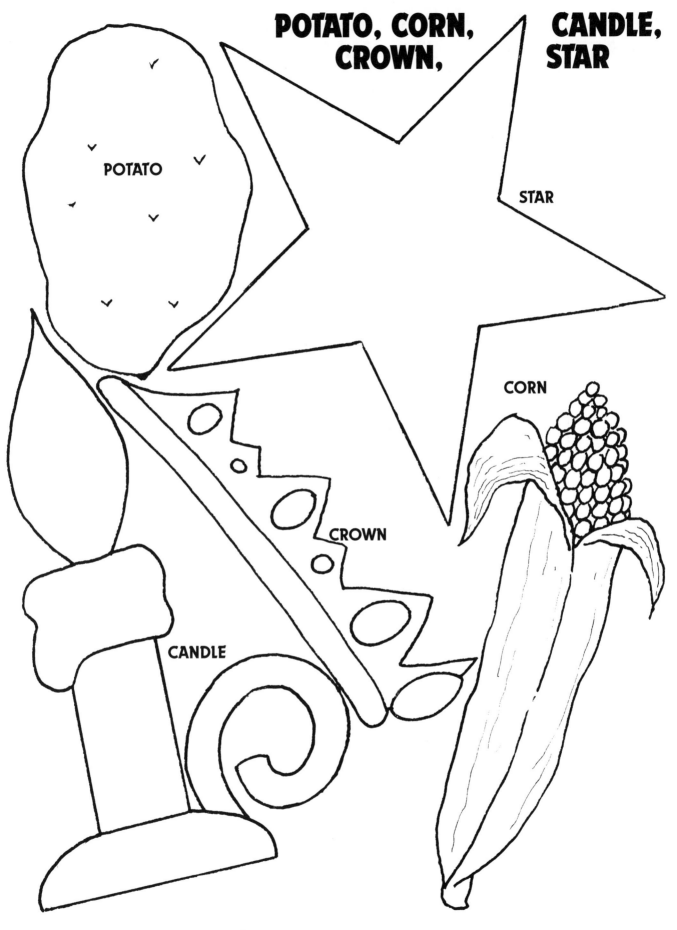

POTATO

STAR

CORN

CROWN

CANDLE

GRAPES, SAUCER, SEAT BELT, IN-LINE SKATES, CANTALOUPE

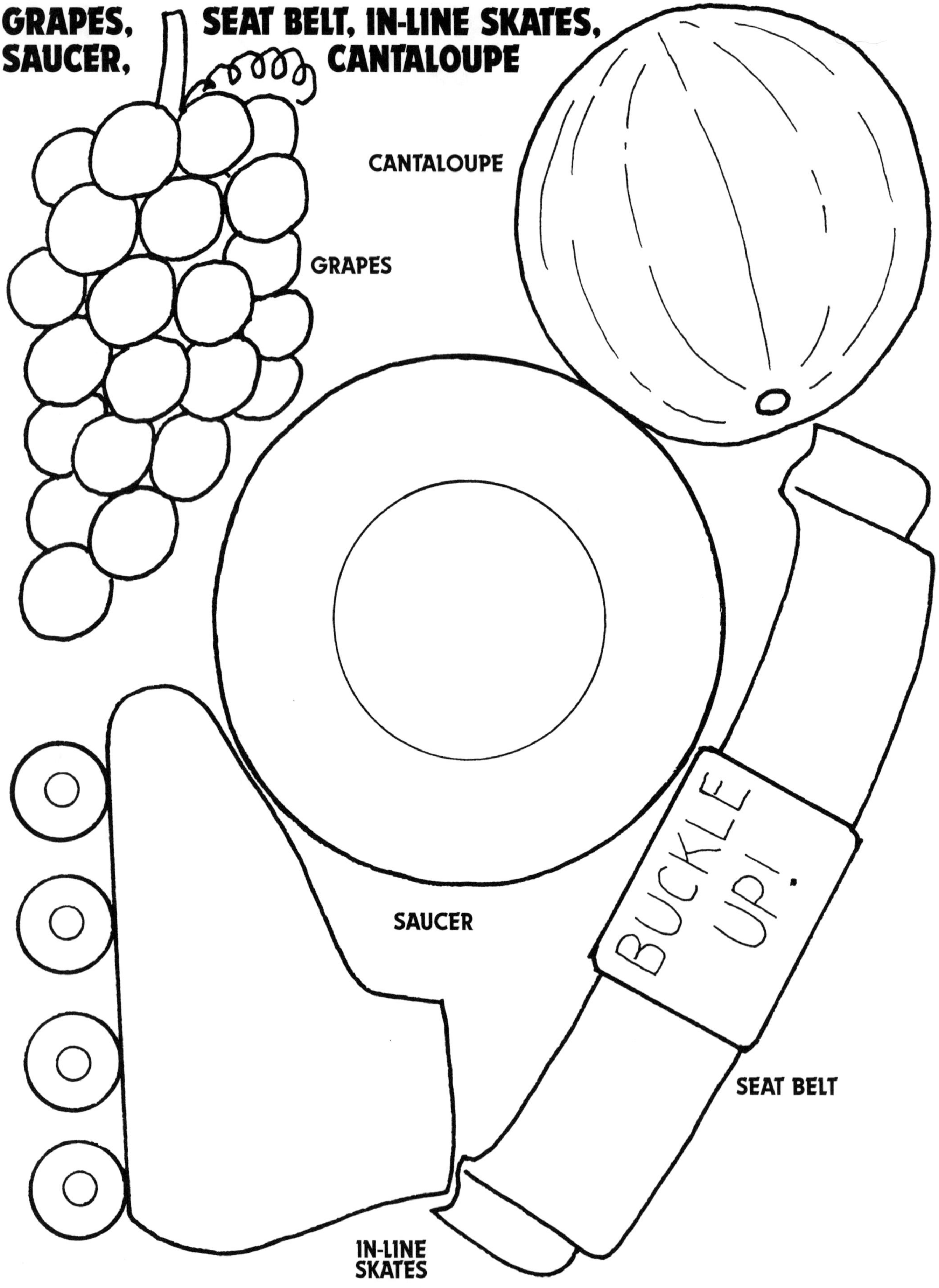

CANTALOUPE

GRAPES

SAUCER

BUCKLE UP!

SEAT BELT

IN-LINE SKATES

110

WASHER, RACCOON, BLACK WALNUT, COTTONWOOD LEAF, IN-LINE SKATES, MAPLE LEAF

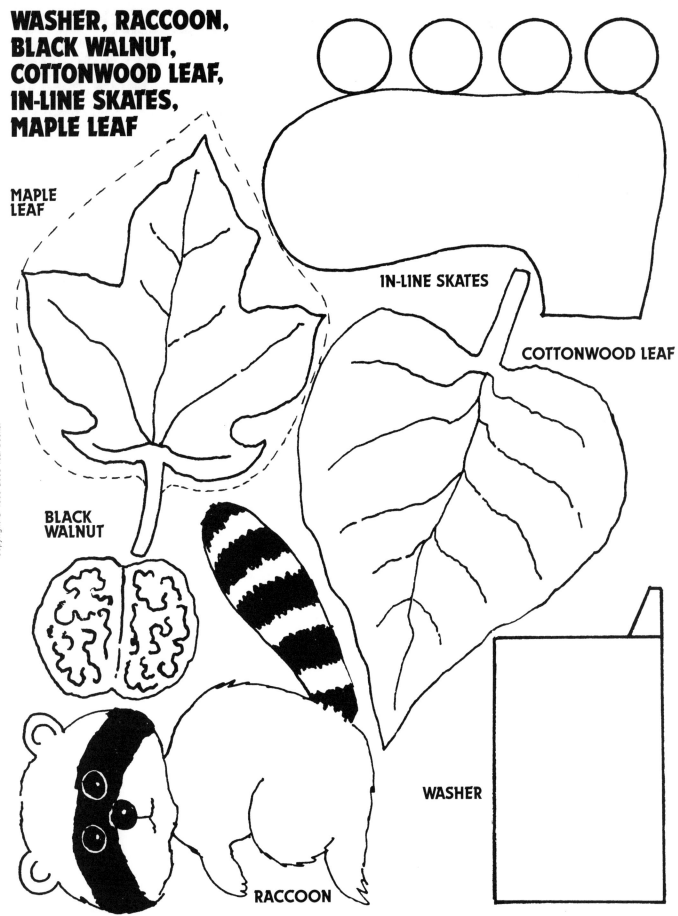

MAPLE LEAF

IN-LINE SKATES

COTTONWOOD LEAF

BLACK WALNUT

WASHER

RACCOON

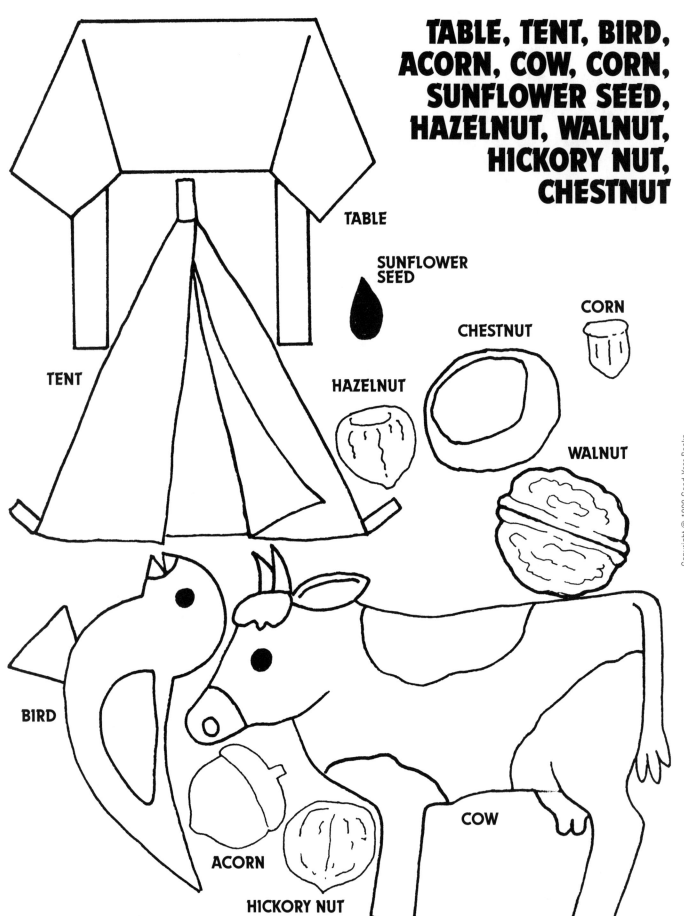

TABLE, TENT, BIRD, ACORN, COW, CORN, SUNFLOWER SEED, HAZELNUT, WALNUT, HICKORY NUT, CHESTNUT

TABLE

SUNFLOWER SEED

CORN

CHESTNUT

TENT

HAZELNUT

WALNUT

BIRD

COW

ACORN

HICKORY NUT

CHILDREN, BOOKCASE, BALL, DOLL, TRUCK, DUST CLOTH, WINDOW, BATHROOM SINK, TOY BOX, TRASH BAG, TRASH CAN

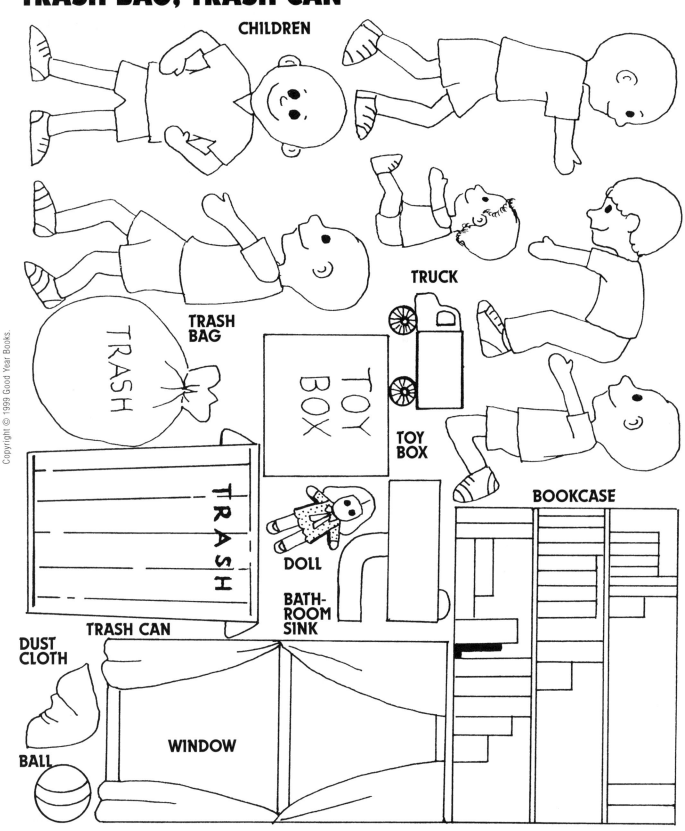

CHILDREN

TRUCK

TRASH BAG

TOY BOX

TOY BOX

BOOKCASE

TRASH

DOLL

BATH-ROOM SINK

TRASH CAN

DUST CLOTH

WINDOW

BALL

HUTCH, CAR, CEILING LAMP, BED, CHAIR, REFRIGERATOR

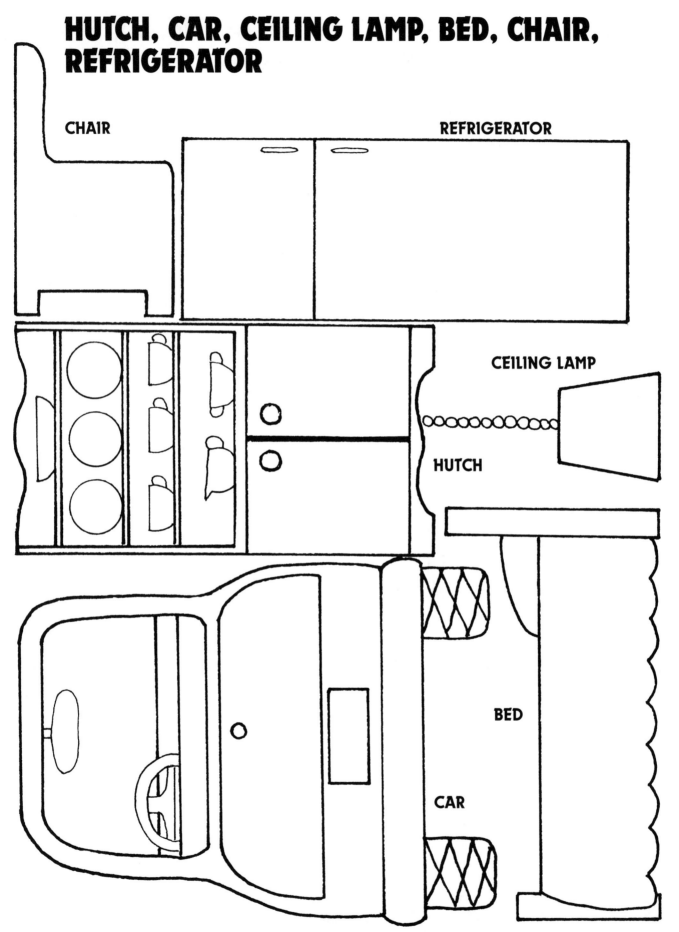

CHAIR

REFRIGERATOR

CEILING LAMP

HUTCH

BED

CAR

CUPBOARD, TABLE, BATHTUB, BICYCLE, PET FOOD, DOG, CAT, MOP, BROOM, RAINDROP, HANGER, CLOUD

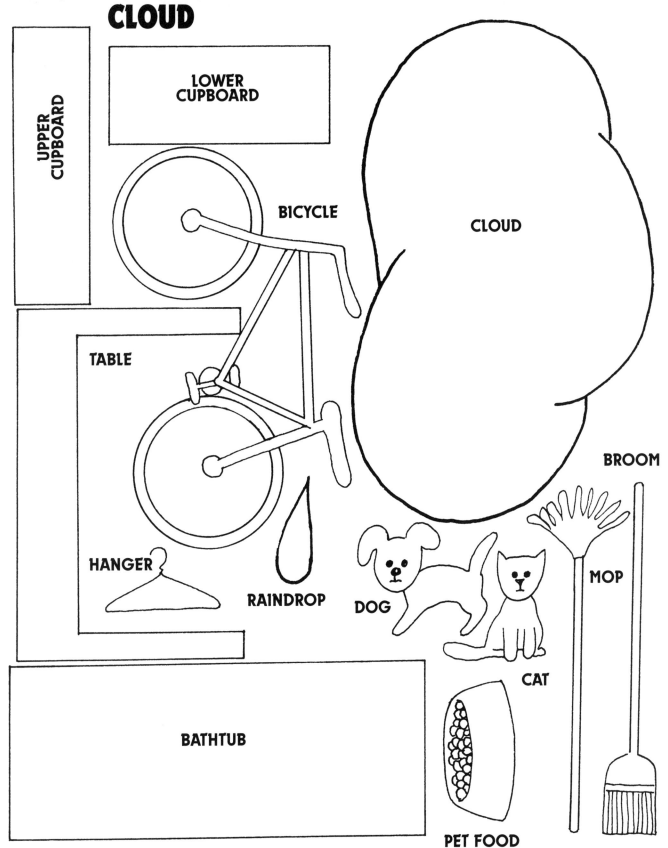

UPPER CUPBOARD

LOWER CUPBOARD

BICYCLE

CLOUD

TABLE

BROOM

HANGER

MOP

RAINDROP

DOG

CAT

BATHTUB

PET FOOD

BODY, SHOES, LEGS

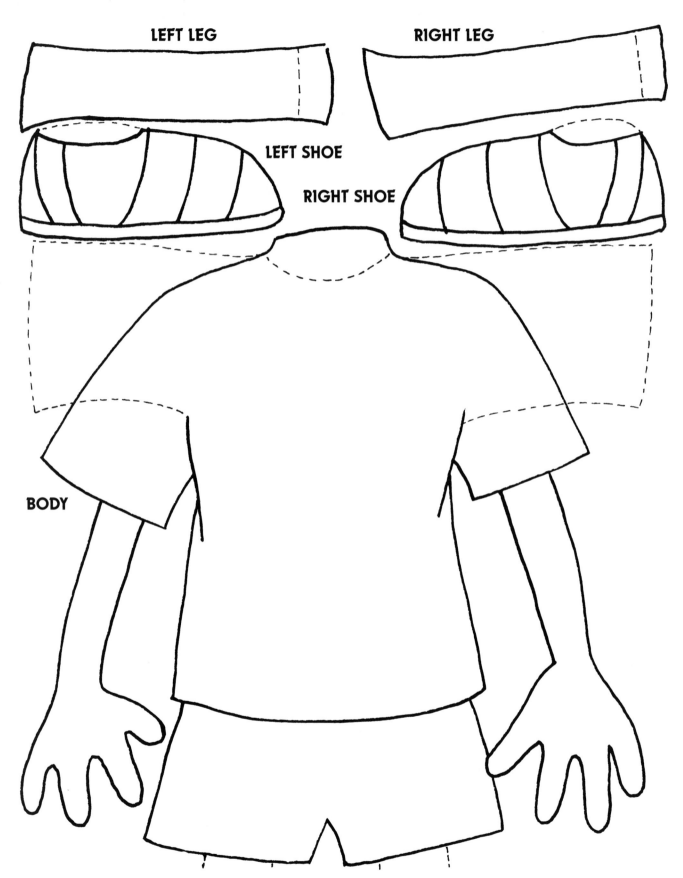

LEFT LEG

RIGHT LEG

LEFT SHOE

RIGHT SHOE

BODY

BORDERS

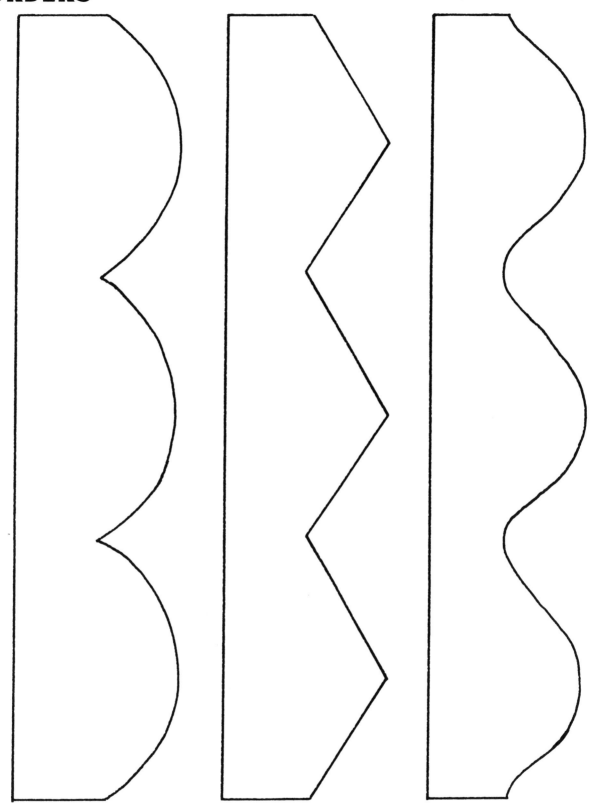

MATERIALS AND SUPPLIES

- any paper—e.g., construction paper, typing paper, wrapping paper, wallpaper, newspaper (or painted newspaper), grocery bags, table paper, shelf paper
- broad-tip marker (optional, for outlining edges)
- scissors

LARGE LETTERS

MATERIALS AND SUPPLIES

- any paper—e.g., construction paper, typing paper, wrapping paper, wallpaper, newspaper (or painted newspaper), grocery bags, table paper, shelf paper
- scissors

SMALL LETTERS

ABCDE
FGHIJK
LMNOP
QRSTU
VWXYZ

MATERIALS AND SUPPLIES

- any paper—e.g., construction paper, typing paper, wrapping paper, wallpaper, newspaper (or painted newspaper), grocery bags, table paper, shelf paper
- scissors